THE LIGHT OF HOPE

THE LIGHT OF HOPE

Vaughn J. Featherstone

Covenant Communications, Inc.

Cover image *Angels of Christmas* © Greg Olsen, Courtesy of Greg Olsen Art, LLC.
For Print information call 1.208.888.2585

Cover design by Christina Ashby © 2007 by Covenant Communications, Inc.

Published by Covenant Communications, Inc.
American Fork, Utah

Copyright © 2007 by Vaughn J. Featherstone

All rights reserved. No part of this book may be reproduced in any format or in any medium without the written permission of the publisher, Covenant Communications, Inc., P.O. Box 416, American Fork, UT 84003. This work is not an official publication of The Church of Jesus Christ of Latter-day Saints. The views expressed within this work are the sole responsibility of the author and do not necessarily reflect the position of The Church of Jesus Christ of Latter-day Saints, Covenant Communications, Inc., or any other entity.

Printed in Canada
First Printing: October 2007

11 10 09 08   10 9 8 7 6 5 4 3 2

ISBN 13: 978-1-59811-455-3
ISBN 10: 1-59811-455-7

Dedicated to all those who truly put Christ in Christmas,
and to all good mothers who understand the value
of the gifts that matter most.

Thanks to Kathy Jenkins for her careful and masterful
job of editing. Also, I personally express my gratitude
for all of Kathy's encouragement and support.

TABLE OF CONTENTS

Hush, My Child. 1
Luke 2:1-14. 3
A Christmas Coat and Six Gifts for Christmas. 9
A Quiet Place Called Bethlehem 37
The Light of Christ Is Christmas 39
Unto the Least of These 43
The Greatest Gifts of All 51
A Christmas Hymn 67
The Light of Hope. 69
Some of Them Do Sparkle 83
Tom: The Orphan Christmas. 93
Sub for Santa 99
At Christmas Time. 107
Christmas Everywhere 109
The Infant King. 117
Christmas—Illusion or Reality? 119
Maybe a Christmas Tree. 141
Purity in Christmas 147
The Christmas Spirit Carries On 157
Closer to Christ at Christmas. 159
A Cradle for Christmas 165

On Christmas Night 175
The Dear Christ Enters In 177
The Gift of Christmas Letters 183
Who Takes the Son Gets It All 193

HUSH, MY CHILD

The heavens split wide, and choirs sang,
    And wise men knelt, and church bells rang;
The shepherds watched in tender care,
    And Mary gave birth to child there.
And angels sang hosannas clear
    While peaceful lay the Christ child near;
Suffused in light's resplendent glow,
    'Twas Mother Mary humming low.

The tune she hummed in tones so clear
    That all inclined a listening ear:
Hush, my child, tonight you rest,
    The world through you will soon be blessed;
So rest, sweet Jesus, sleep awhile,
    And feel the warmth of Father's smile,
For holy art thou, oh little one,
    Only begotten King and Son.

LUKE 2:1-14

Born of gentle parents, Luke practiced medicine; he is mentioned in the fourth chapter of Colossians, where he is described as the beloved physician. Paul describes him along with Marcus, Aristarchus, and Demas as fellow laborers. Luke was the writer of the gospel of Luke and the book of Acts. Joseph Smith's translation attributes to Luke a high calling as a "messenger of Jesus Christ." We read the second chapter of Luke from the writings of a gentle soul to Gentile readers:

> AND it came to pass in those days, that there went out a decree from Caesar Augustus, that all the world should be taxed.
>
> (And this taxing was first made when Cyrenius was governor of Syria.)
>
> And all went to be taxed, every one into his own city.
>
> And Joseph also went up from Galilee, out of the city of Nazareth, into Judaea, unto the city of

David, which is called Bethlehem; (because he was of the house and lineage of David) (Luke 2:1-4).

The prophet Micah wrote, "But thou, Bethlehem Ephratah, [though] thou be little among the thousands of Judah, [yet] out of thee shall he come forth unto me [that is] to be ruler in Israel; whose goings forth [have been] from of old, from everlasting" (Micah 5:2).

And John confirms both Luke and Micah with his declaration, "Hath not the scripture said, That Christ cometh of the seed of David, and out of the town of Bethlehem, where David was?" (John 7:42).

Leaving Galilee, Joseph went "to be taxed with Mary his espoused wife, being great with child" (Luke 2:5). As a physician, Luke undoubtedly knew how difficult it would have been for Mary to travel to Bethlehem, regardless of whether she was walking or riding a donkey. (Doctors today counsel women not to travel in cars or on planes during the last month or two before the baby is due.) Luke would have been concerned not only because of the physical stress of travel, but because this was Mary's first child. He would have known the quiet fear she carried into the unknown as they made their way along the dusty road.

> And so it was, that, while they were there, the days were accomplished that she should be delivered.
>
> And she brought forth her firstborn son, and wrapped him in swaddling clothes, and laid him in a manger; because there was no room for them in the inn (Luke 2:6-7).

Luke naturally saw through the eyes of a physician, with which he had compassion regarding the travails of delivering a first child. But I believe that he also considered the traditional birthright blessings and had a special understanding of the doctrine of the firstborn, especially in the Savior's case.

In the patriarchal order, the "firstborn son" is considered the heir, and as such he inherits leadership of the family when the father dies. In this case, the Father was God. Jesus was the firstborn of the spirit children of our Heavenly Father, and as the Only Begotten of the Father in the flesh, so He received His Father's birthright.

One wonders how often Luke had delivered babies; it stands to reason that his patients were very often the poor, who had nothing but swaddling clothes in which to wrap the newborn child. None of the other gospel writers refer to the swaddling clothes, and they provide few details about circumstances surrounding the humble birth. But Luke, with his unique experiences as a physician, could envision not only the full birth process, but the Christ Child clothed from His nakedness and laid in a manger. As he reflected on his own experiences at the bedside of laboring mothers, I imagine it must have hurt Luke to consider that there was no room at the inn.

> And there were in the same country shepherds abiding in the field, keeping watch over their flock by night (Luke 2:8).

Although Luke did not mention the star, he must have been aware of it. Its radiant beams must have illuminated Luke's heart as it does ours today; as with us, he must have felt its profound message. Of all the creations of God, one star set in motion by His Almighty hand had the sacred privilege of announcing Christ's birth. No wonder the star over Bethlehem shone so brightly! It still shines today for those who believe.

Imagine the wonder of the shepherds as they beheld the star and witnessed all the glorious events connected with the Savior's birth:

> And, lo, the angel of the Lord came upon them, and the glory of the Lord shone round about them: and they were sore afraid (Luke 2:9).

Luke must have imagined, as we do, the shepherds cowering amid their flocks, filled with a pronounced combination of fright and awe as the glory of the Lord surrounded them. With Luke, the shepherds—and all of mankind—thrill with the message:

> And the angel said unto them, Fear not: for, behold, I bring you good tidings of great joy, which shall be to all people (Luke 2:10).

What excitement to hear good tidings of great joy to all people. We know that Luke was not there that night; we imagine that he must have heard the tales from the shepherds. But we also know that some things we experience vicariously could not be more real. How Luke's heart must have rejoiced as he heard the breathless shepherds recounting the amazing occurrence.

As he pondered the events that happened that night, Luke must have wondered which of all the angels of heaven had the sacred privilege of declaring:

For unto you is born this day in the city of David a Saviour, which is Christ the Lord.

And this *shall be* a sign unto you; Ye shall find the babe wrapped in swaddling clothes, lying in a manger.

And suddenly there was with the angel a multitude of the heavenly host praising God, and saying,

Glory to God in the highest, and on earth peace, good will toward men (Luke 2:11-14).

To Luke, the gentle physician, we owe much of our knowledge about that sacred night when the Savior of all mankind left the realms of heaven and entered mortality—announced by the brightest star in the galaxy, hailed by the voice of an angel, and cradled in the humble surroundings of a manger. We can be grateful for his sensitive details, words that have become tradition in countless Christian homes. This year, as you contemplate the wonder of the Christmas story, remember a gentle physician who reflected on his years of experience to bring us the sweetest details of the greatest story ever told.

A CHRISTMAS COAT AND SIX GIFTS FOR CHRISTMAS

Christmas is a glorious time of the year—yet for many, Christmas is a sorrowful, heart-wrenching experience. While many anticipate its arrival with joy, some anticipate it with deep agony, because it reminds them of what they do not have. It is a sad time for many who have lost loved ones, for others who have wayward children, and for some whose companions are unfaithful. It is difficult, too, for those surrounded by the thankless. It is a challenging time for the unemployed and the poor, who have no money with which to buy gifts. Some who are heavily indebted see it as just another burdensome trial. Christmas can also be painful for those who have debilitating diseases, the selfish, the unloved, the orphaned, and the widowed.

Yet to those with faith, Christmas is a time when hope shines brightest. Christmas should be a season of healing. Perhaps it has most to do with our own attitudes: the selfish can never be satisfied, because they will always want more, but those who are thoughtful, selfless, and caring will always be rich.

Those who focus on Christ will have a sweet, memorable Christmas. As we reflect over the years, the Christmases we remember most clearly and with the greatest fondness aren't those in which we received the greatest number of beribboned packages from under the tree. Instead, they are the Christmases that were touched by the true Spirit of Christ—those seasons in which we focused on Him.

How, then, do we invite that Spirit into our homes and our hearts? I would suggest that we should consider six gifts at this Christmas season—gifts that will invite the spirit of Christmas and create the most memorable holiday regardless of the personal or financial circumstances in which we find ourselves.

The Gift of Self

Though it is one of the most important gifts, the gift of self may be most difficult of all gifts to give.

The playwright Moss Hart related an experience in his young life when his family was suffering desperately:

> Obviously Christmas was out of the question—we were barely staying alive. On Christmas Eve my father was very silent during the evening meal. Then he surprised and startled me by turning to me and saying, "Let's take a walk." He had never suggested such a thing before, and moreover it was a very cold winter's night. I was even more surprised when he said as we left the house, "Let's go down to 149th Street and Westchester Avenue." My heart leapt within me. That was the section where all the big stores were, where at Christmas time open pushcarts full of toys stood packed end-to-end for blocks at a stretch. On other Christmas Eves I had often gone there with my aunt, and from our tour of the carts she had gathered what I

wanted the most. My father had known of this, of course, and I joyously concluded that this walk could mean only one thing—he was going to buy me a Christmas present.

On the walk down I was beside myself with delight and an inner relief. It has been a bad year for me, that year of my aunt's going, and I wanted a Christmas present terribly—not merely a present, but a symbol, a token of some sort. I needed some sign from my father or mother that they knew what I was going through and cared for me as much as my aunt and grandfather did. I am sure they were giving me what mute signs they could, but I did not see them. The idea that my father had managed a Christmas present for me in spite of everything filled me with a sudden peace and lightness of heart I had not known in months.

We hurried on, our heads bent against the wind, to the cluster of lights ahead that was 149th Street and Westchester Avenue, and those lights seemed to me the brightest lights I had ever seen. Tugging at my father's coat, I started down the line of pushcarts. There were all kinds of things that I wanted, but since nothing had been said by my father about buying a present, I would merely pause before a pushcart to say, with as much control as I could muster, "Look at that chemistry set!" or "There's a stamp album!" or "Look at the printing press!" Each time my father would pause and ask the pushcart man the price. Then without a word we would move on to the next pushcart. Once or twice he would pick up a toy of some kind and look at it and then at me, as if to suggest this might be something I might like, but I was ten years old and a good deal beyond just a toy; my heart was set on a chemistry set or a printing press. There they were on every pushcart we stopped at but the price was always the same and soon I looked up and saw we were nearing the end of the line. Only two or three more pushcarts remained. My father looked up, too, and I heard him jingle some coins in his pocket. In a flash I knew it all. He'd gotten together about seventy-five cents to buy me a Christmas present, and he hadn't dared say so in case there was nothing to be had for so small a sum.

As I looked up at him, I saw a look of despair and disappointment in his eyes that brought me closer to him than I had ever been in my life. I wanted to throw my arms around him and say, "It doesn't matter . . . I understand. . . this is better than a chemistry set or a printing press . . . I love you."

But instead we stood shivering beside each other for a moment then turned away from the last two pushcarts and started silently back home. I don't know why the words remained choked up within me. I didn't even take his hand on the way home nor did he take mine. We were not on that basis. Nor did I ever tell him how close to him I felt that night—that for a little while the concrete wall between father and son had crumbled away and I knew that we were two lonely people struggling to reach each other. I came close to telling him many years later, but again the moment passed.

Contrast the experience of young Moss Hart to that of a young Bishop Thomas S. Monson. Years ago we both attended a Scouting meeting in Washington, D.C. He invited me to his room to prepare for part of the conference. We talked about Scout business for some time, and then, for the next two hours, we just visited.

He told of the time when he was a young bishop of a ward in Salt Lake City; there were 89 widows in that ward. During all the years that he was bishop—and during all the years that followed—he had delivered a stewing hen or box of chocolates to each one of those widows. I was so touched at the tender way in which he related many of the experiences that happened during his visits. How those sweet sisters must have looked forward to spending time with him! With moistened eyes, he told me, "There are only thirteen widows left." In speaking of men like President Thomas S. Monson, Ridgewell Cullen wrote, "Here was a man of that unusual caliber which must ultimately make him a leader of men in whatever walk of life he chose for that strenuous journey." What a blessing it is when we can truly give of self and reach out to others.

I have had many memorable Christmases in my life, but one particularly comes to mind. I was a senior in high school; my older brother had married, and Mom was working full-time, which I think she did from the time she and Dad were separated. My younger brother Jim and I both sang in the a cappella choir at South High School under Armont Willardsen; we had such confidence in him that all of us thought he should have directed the Mormon Tabernacle Choir. As the Christmas season approached, our choir had many singing engagements. A few were outside, but most were in chapels.

Our family was always pressed financially. My older brother had a dark blue shirt of good quality material; I wore it so often, he finally let me have it. I wore either that shirt or a white T-shirt every day to school. Each night, I washed and ironed that navy blue shirt so it would be ready for the next day.

As Christmas approached, I hoped I could somehow get a new winter coat. The only coat I had to shelter me against the winter cold was a sport coat a neighbor had given us—and I remember how embarrassed I felt whenever our choir sang outside. On one occasion we sang at the monument in Sugarhouse. It was cold, overcast, and snowing—but as cold as I was, that was nothing compared to my embarrassment. Many in the choir asked, "Aren't you cold?" I responded cheerfully, "Gosh, no, I am fine!" I'm sure no one believed me—the weather was bitter.

That year I asked my mom for a new coat. Somehow, even though I knew our finances were meager, I thought my need warranted a new coat. I worked part-time in a grocery store after school and gave my mother almost my entire paycheck, keeping out only $2 a week for school lunches and other expenses. It took almost all the money Mother and I made to pay the mortgage payment and utilities, buy food, and take care of other necessities.

As Christmas neared, I remember the other five children also putting in their orders for Christmas. But I thought that surely, after all I had given to Mother for the family, she would buy me a new coat. I was the senior class president at our high school, and I was constantly embarrassed that I did not have a coat. Even though I was acutely aware of our family's financial condition, I thought I deserved a new coat. All my hope and self-worth hinged on whether I got the coat. For me, at that time, it was more than physical need—it was something I longed for, and it somehow indicated that I was worthwhile.

Christmas morning, we awoke early and ran to the living room. I searched near my stocking, which was filled to overflowing—and though there were some less expensive gifts there (all my mother could afford, I'm sure), there was no sign of a new coat. I thought for a moment my heart would break.

As I reveled in my despair, suddenly I realized how selfish I had been. I had barely considered what my younger brothers and sisters had asked for, and my thoughts turned to their needs. One of my sisters had asked for a watch but had not received it. I remember trying to help the younger ones understand that Mom had done all she could.

Mother did not get up with us; she usually came out a little later. By the time she joined us, my disappointment had vanished to the point that a new coat would have seemed almost like a transgression. I had thought about my mother, lying in bed, her heart breaking, knowing that six children would be disappointed on the one day when hope shined the brightest. This wonderful, noble woman suffered much during her lifetime, but I believe that Christmases during these years when her children were young brought the greatest suffering. It must have been difficult for her to come out and face us, but somehow she did.

Somehow she managed to put on a big smile and make a great fuss over the things Santa had brought us, never revealing the heaviness of her aching heart. It was then that I first saw and truly comprehended the smallest glimpse of a mother's love.

The little gifts we made for Mom at Primary and school were all she received that year. She made each one of us feel that those gifts were more precious than diamonds and rubies. She hung our creations on the wall and placed them on shelves, treating each one as if they were very valuable.

That Christmas was so memorable for me because it was the year I finally grew up. I began to have empathy for those who suffered—to forget what I wanted and to help the others around me find happiness, just as my mother had always done. Giving the gift of self, becoming truly selfless, can help all of us have a merry Christmas regardless of whether there are gifts.

The Gift of Love

Charity has been defined as the pure love of Christ. When I was ordained a bishop and called to the Presiding Bishopric, President Harold B. Lee laid his hands on my head and said, "Whenever you are faced with a problem, ask yourself what the Master would do as measured by his teaching, and then do it." Hardly a day has gone by since then that I have not asked myself that question.

A national women's magazine retold a Christmas event that illustrates the amazing power of love:

> It was but a few short days until Christmas in 1966. Two young Elders of the Mormon Church

walked the streets of Laredo, Texas, knocking on doors in search of someone who would listen to their gospel message. No one, it seemed, in the entire city had time to hear the teachings of the Savior, so intent were they that the celebration of His birth should suit their own social purposes.

Filled with discouragement, the two young men turned their backs to the approaching twilight and began the long walk home. Retracing their steps of the afternoon, they came upon a low, windswept riverbank. Jutting from its brow stood the barest means of shelter, constructed of weathered wooden slats and large pieces of cardboard. Strangely, they felt moved to go to the door and knock. A small, olive-skinned child with tangled back hair and large dark eyes answered. Her mother appeared behind her, a short, thin woman with a tired but warm smile. In her rich Spanish alto she invited the young men to come in and rest awhile. They were made welcome and seated on the clean-swept floor. The little one-room shanty seemed to be filled with shy, smiling, dark-eyed children. The mother proudly introduced each of them—eight in all—and each in turn quickly bobbed his or her head.

The young men were deeply moved at the extreme poverty they saw. Not one in the family had shoes, and their clothes were ill-fitting and in a condition beyond mending. The walls of the little home showed daylight between the wooden slats, and eight little rolls of bedding were pressed tightly into the cracks to help keep out the draft until they were needed for sleeping. A small round fire pit dug in one corner marked the kitchen. An odd assortment of chipped dishes and pots were stacked beside an old ice chest, and a curtained-off section with a cracked porcelain tub served as the bathing area. Except for these, the room was barren.

The mother told how her husband had gone north to find employment. He had written that he had found a job of manual labor and that it took most of his small wage to pay his board and room. But, she told the young men, he had managed to save fifty cents to send them for Christmas, with which she had purchased two boxes of fruit gelatin. It was one of the children's favorites and would make a special treat on Christmas day.

Later, long after the young men had left the family, they still asked each other incredulously, "Fifty cents? . . . fifty cents for eight children for Christmas?" Surely there must be something they could do to brighten Christmas for such children.

The next morning, as soon as the local shops opened, the young men hurried to the dime store and purchased as many crayons, cars, trucks and little inexpensive toys as they could afford. Each was carefully wrapped in brightly colored paper and all were put in a large grocery bag. That evening the two young men took their gifts to the shanty on the riverbank. When they knocked, the mother swung the door open wide and invited them in. They stepped inside and in halting Spanish explained to the children that they had seen Santa, and he had been in such a hurry he'd asked if they would deliver his gifts to the children for him.

With cries of delight the children scrambled for the bag, spilling its contents upon the floor and quickly dividing the treasured packages. Silently the mother's eyes filled with tears of gratitude. She stepped forward to clasp tightly one of each of the young men's hands in hers. For long moments she was unable to speak. Then, with tears still welling from her eyes, she smiled and said, "No one ever has been so kind. You have given us a special gift, the kind of love that lights Christmas in the heart. May we also give you a special gift?" From the corner of the room she drew out the two small boxes of fruit gelatin and handed them to the young men. Then all eyes were moist. All knew the true meaning of giving, and none would forget that at Christmas the greatest gift of all was given (*Women's Day*, Dec. 18, 1979).

At a time like this, I remember the words of "A Poor Wayfaring Man of Grief":

A poor wayfaring man of grief
Hath often crossed me on my way
Who sued so humbly for relief
That I could never answer nay.
I had not pow'r to ask his name,
Where-to he went, or whence he came;
Yet there was something in his eye
That won my love; I knew not why.

We will always have the poor among us; to care, to share, and to love is essential to our own eternal progress. Mother Teresa demonstrated our responsibility in these words as she received the Nobel Peace Prize.

> The poor are very wonderful people. One evening we went out and we picked up four people from the street. And one of them was in a most terrible condition—and I told the sisters: You take care of the other three, I take care of this one that looked worse. So I did for her all that my love can do. I put her in bed, and there was such a beautiful smile on her face. She took hold of my hand, as she said one word only: Thank-you—and she died.
>
> I could not help but examine my conscience before her, and I asked what would I say if I was in her place. And my answer was very simple. I would have tried to draw a little attention to myself. I would have said I am hungry, that I am dying, I am

cold, I am in pain, or something, but she gave me much more—she gave me her grateful love. And she died with a smile on her face. . . .

[We picked up a man] from the drain, half eaten with worms, and we brought him to the home. "I have lived like an animal in the street, but I am going to die like an angel, loved and cared for." And it was so wonderful to see the greatness of that man who could speak like that, who could die like that without blaming anybody, without cursing anybody, without comparing anything. Like an angel—this is the greatness of our people. And that is why we believe that Jesus has said: I was hungry—I was naked—I was homeless—I was unwanted, unloved, uncared for—and you did it to me. I want you to find the poor here, right in your own home first. And begin love there. Be that good news to your own people. And find out about your next-door neighbor—do you know who they are?

I had the most extraordinary experience with a Hindu family who had eight children. A gentleman came to our house and said: "Mother Teresa, there is a family with eight children, they had not eaten for so long—do something." So I took some rice, and I went there immediately. And I saw the children—their eyes shining with hunger—I don't know if you have ever seen hunger. But I have seen it very often.

> And she took the rice, she divided the rice and she went out. When she came back, I asked her—where did you go, what did you do? And she gave me a very simple answer: "They are hungry also." What struck me most was that she knew [a Moslem family that was also hungry]. . . . I didn't bring more rice that evening because I wanted them to enjoy the joy of sharing. But there were those children, radiating joy, sharing the joy with their mother because she had the love to give. And you see this is where love begins—at home.

Even the poor in their poverty are expected to give. Many of the most touching Christmas stories—the classics—provide for us a glimpse at those who seem to have nothing, yet share all they have with another. The Master so often ministered to the poor; He assured us that the meek, the merciful, the pure in heart, and the poor in spirit are among the most blessed.

French scientist René de Chardin wrote, "Some day after we have mastered the winds, the waves, the tides, and gravity, we will harness for God the energies of love. Then for the second time in the history of the world, man will have discovered fire."

The Gift of Time

A few years ago, I was working at the office a few days before Christmas. As I sat behind the desk I received several calls—and within just a few minutes, all my afternoon meetings were cancelled. I suddenly had four precious hours in which to work on the matters that were piling up on my desk. At once the happy thought occurred to me: "If I can get all this work done, I won't have to come in during the holidays!"

Within seconds, a different, more sober thought occurred to me. "If Jesus were here and suddenly had four hours," I wondered, "would he do paperwork, or would he go visit the widows?" I knew what I had to do. I picked up some gifts from around the office, gathered up some books and other things, and set out on my visits.

As I knocked on the first widow's door, she welcomed me inside; when I asked how she was doing, she responded, "I'm doing all right." Something deep inside me revealed that she *wasn't* doing well. I pursued, asking, "How are you *really* doing?"

She began to cry, and answered, "I don't have any money with which to pay my rent this month." Each Christmas, a friend of mine gives me several $100 bills to distribute to those who are in need. I still had one of the bills left; I pulled my wallet out of my pocket, drew out the $100 bill, and handed it to her. She wept, and I wept. As I walked down the hall after our visit, I thought, "What if I hadn't come?"

The next home I visited was that of Louise Lake, a woman who had been in a wheelchair for thirty-seven years. Her nurse welcomed me in and asked me to wait in the living room. She was gone for about five minutes—possibly fluffing the pillow, brushing out Louise's hair, or applying a little bit of makeup. When I was invited to her bedroom, I learned that Louise had pneumonia, and she was on oxygen. I sat down by her on the bed. We visited, held hands for a few moments, and then she said, "Do you know what I'd like to have more than anything else in this world?"

"What?" I asked.

"I wish I could get a message to President Kimball," she whispered.

"You can," I assured her. "I'll write it for you. You tell me what you want to say to him, and I'll make some notes. I think I can translate my notes back into English and get a letter off to President Kimball for you."

I will never forget her message. I could hardly see the page through my tears as I recorded her simple words: "President Kimball, I have been in a wheelchair for thirty-seven years, and I have never murmured once. I have taken everything that the Lord dished out, and I'll take whatever He dishes out as long as He wants to dish it out. I will not murmur. . . . I have been in great pain—pain beyond belief—but the wonderful thing about pain is that once it is gone, you do not remember how bad it was. So when it comes again, you don't know how bad it is going to get." Then, with a sparkle in her eye, she said, "Please tell President Kimball that I have my hat in my hand, and I am ready to go whenever the Lord will come after me."

As we concluded our visit, I asked Louise if she would like a blessing. We were both in tears throughout a beautiful blessing from her Heavenly Father. As she regained her composure, she told me, "Elder Featherstone, at a very early hour this morning I had a dream that was so real that I was awakened. I called my nurse in and told her, 'I just had a dream that one of the General Authorities was coming to my home to give me a special blessing, and he would come today.' The dream was so real that I said to my nurse, 'We'd better prepare, because he will be here.' So I knew you were coming."

As I left Louise's apartment, I was overcome by the greatest possible love for the Lord. Imagine that He would use me, that He knew me by name! I knew then who had cancelled my appointments.

I love the Lord for many things, but I especially love Him for trusting me with such a sacred experience and somehow knowing that I would respond in the right way.

The gift of time is one of the most precious we can give.

The Gift of Service

President Harold B. Lee told the following story at a Regional Representative meeting:

> I became a president of a stake in my "almost" youthful days, in my early thirties, with a stake of 7,200 to 7,400 members in 11 wards. It was out in the southwest part of this city where most of those in industrial pursuits lived. I remember one Christmas, I think it was the first Christmas after I was made stake president. Our little girls had opened their Christmas morning gifts and dashed over to show their little friends a new doll and whatever else they had, and shortly they came back, both of them crying. "What in the world is the matter?" we asked. They said, "Well, we were over to our friends, and they didn't have any Christmas. Santa Claus did not come to their place." And all too late we remembered that just across the street was a family where the father was not a member of the Church. The children were, the mother passively so, but the father had been out of work, and we had forgotten. Our Christmas

was spoiled. We sent for the children and tried to divide what we had to try to make up for our lack of thoughtfulness, but it was too late, and Christmas dinner that day did not taste very good to me. I was unhappy. I did not sleep well because I was in charge of the welfare of my people.

So we made a survey, and to our amazement we found that 4,800 out of our 7,200 to 7,400 were either wholly or partially dependent. There was no government work in those days. We only had to look to ourselves, and Church finances were falling off. We were told we couldn't look for much help from the general funds of the Church. Thus were we situated as we approached another Christmas season.

We found we had 1,000 children under 10 years of age, for whom, without someone to help them, there would be no Christmas. Then we started to prepare on the second floor of our old storehouse on Pierpont Street. We gathered up the toys—all the broken toys—and for a month or two before Christmas all the fathers and mothers were there making toys, many for their own children. If you wanted to get the spirit of Christmas, you only had to step in and see that. We started out then to see to it that none of the 1,000 children would be without a Christmas.

The Light of Hope

There would be a Christmas dinner in all the homes of those 4,800 who, without our help, wouldn't have any nuts, candy, oranges, a roast of beef or meat of some kind with all that went with it for Christmas. It was on the day before Christmas, and I was then a City Commissioner. We had a heavy snow storm, and I had been out all night with the crews trying to get the streets cleared, knowing that I would be to blame if any of my men fell down. I went home to get cleaned up to go back to the office, and as I started back to town there was a little boy thumbing his way into town. I took him into the car and I said, "Son, are you ready for Christmas?" "Oh, gee, mister, we aren't going to have any Christmas at our home. Daddy died three months ago and left Mama and me and a little brother and sister under 10 years of age." "Where are you going, son?" "I am going up to a free picture show." I turned the heat on in the car and said, "Now give me your name and address." They were not members of the Church.

"Somebody will come to your home; you won't be forgotten. Now you have a good time today." That night I asked every bishop to go out with his deliverymen and see that every family was cared for. They were all to report back. I had forgotten this little boy to whom I had made a promise. I had been so busy I had forgotten this little family. I asked the bishop if he had any more gifts left. He said, "Yes, we have." Now, I had promised this little family there would be a Christmas for them. A little later, he called to say they, too, had all been taken care of.

As I awoke that Christmas morning, as I ate my Christmas dinner, in my heart I said: "God grant that I would never let another year pass but that I, as a leader, would know my people. I would know their needs. I would be feeling after the ones who needed most my leadership. My carelessness had meant suffering, because I did not know my people the first year" (Regional Representative Seminar Report).

When I read this account, I decided that is the kind of stake president I would like to be.

While I served as mission president, a good friend sent me five $100 bills to share wherever I felt a need. In one interview with a missionary just before Christmas, I asked him, "How are you doing financially?"

"I am doing the best I can," he answered.

"Are you getting along all right?" I asked.

With great emotion, he responded, "President, I am doing the best I can. There are several other children in the family. My dad is a custodian at the high school, and my mother joined the school lunch program so she could work during the day when the children were away and be home when the children were home. It takes everything both of them earn to support me on a mission."

After pausing for a few seconds, he continued, "President, since I have been a zone leader, I have used a car, and it costs $25 a month to rent the car, plus the money for gasoline. Each month I fall a little further behind. I have tried to hold down my costs." Then, with tears flowing freely, he told me, "President, I haven't eaten for three days trying to hold my costs to a minimum and not ask my parents for any more money. My little sister just had a birthday, and someone gave her a dollar in an envelope. She sent the dollar to me because she thought I might need it more than she did."

I reached into my wallet and pulled out two of the $100 bills and passed them on to this wonderful, sweet elder. That day I witnessed so many acts of service: the friend who gave me money to bless the lives of others; the elder who labored full-time in teaching the gospel; the humble parents who worked so hard to make his mission possible; and the little sister who sacrificed her birthday present for a much-loved brother. What a blessing to serve!

More than two decades ago, President Ezra Taft Benson related the account of a baby in a southern community who fell into a well. The hole was sixty feet deep and only thirteen inches across. None of the men could fit into the hole to rescue the baby; even a circus thin-man volunteered, but his shoulders were too broad.

Then Elbert Gray, a young boy, volunteered. You can imagine how terrifying such a rescue would have been for anyone, but especially for a boy. He was lowered into the well on the end of a rope; sharp rocks tore into his face and his bare feet. He finally reached the baby and managed to grab its shirt, but the cramped position he was in prevented him from getting a good hold. They pulled Elbert back up to the opening of the hole.

Imagine the surprise of the crowd of onlookers when Elbert volunteered to go down again—this time head-first, so he could firmly grasp the child with both hands. Shaking with cold and blood streaming from his numerous injuries, he was lowered head-first into the sixty-foot well. As he was slowly brought back to the surface, he expended all his strength to bring the baby with him.

Elbert Gray—who understood that true service, service that brings the greatest fulfillment, must be voluntary—was awarded a bronze medal, the symbol of heroism, by the Carnegie Fund Hero Commission.

The Gift of Means

The year I was called into the Presiding Bishopric we moved to our present ward, and that Christmas we were asked to contribute to a building fund. We had two sons on missions, our son Joseph was a junior in high school, and the others were younger.

During the family home evening after Thanksgiving, we told the children, "We are supporting two boys on a mission, we have other expenses, and we are not making as much money as we have previously made. So we've got to be very frugal this year. Now we have learned that we have a building fund to take care of. We would like each of you to think of one or two things you really want, and we'll do our best to get them for you." We provided the children with pieces of paper on which to write their wish list and gave them a few minutes to think it over before we collected their notes.

After family home evening, I sat down in the other room to read what the children had written. When I came to Joe's, my heart melted as I read, "Dear Dad, please give my entire Christmas to the building fund."

I sought Joe out and said, "Joe, you can't do that. What do you really want? We'll try to get it for you."

"That's what I really want," he insisted. "I want you to give my Christmas to the building fund."

When I brought the issue up with his mother, she told me, "You can't do that—you can't give his Christmas to the building fund. That's not right; the building fund is *our* responsibility."

As I thought about it, though, I realized that if I were Joseph's age, I would want to do exactly the same thing. So I figured out about what we would have spent on gifts for Joseph, prepared a receipt, and decided I would put it in his stocking late on Christmas Eve.

My wife was greatly troubled over the situation, and the closer it got to Christmas, the more troubled I became as well. Christmas Eve finally arrived, and I remember putting that slip in his stocking along with some candy, nuts, and oranges. That's all he got that year for Christmas. I didn't sleep that night. I started worrying, wondering if he really meant what he told me.

The next morning we faithfully carried out our Christmas tradition: We awakened, cleaned up, and had prayer before going into the living room. My eyes were solely on Joseph. He pulled the receipt out of his stocking and read it, and the tears began to flow. I interpreted those tears as regret on his part—and I could not have been more heartsick.

I didn't have the heart to ask Joseph how he felt. When his friends came over later and asked what he got for Christmas, he replied, "Oh, a slip of paper about this size," gesturing with his hands.

"What was it?" one asked. Joseph showed them the receipt from his stocking.

One of them let out a slow whistle. "Well, that wasn't much of a Christmas, was it?" His question was the one that had filled my troubled heart all morning, so I listened closely for Joseph's answer.

"Actually, it was the best Christmas I ever had in my life," Joseph replied. His humble answer reminded me that the gift of means is sometimes very important.

I remember the story of Abram and Zimri, who worked side-by-side in a field; Abram had a wife and seven sons, and Zimri was single. When harvest time arrived, Abram and Zimri divided the harvest equally.

That night, Abram sat in the warmth of his fire, surrounded by his wife and seven sons, and thought, "I have seven sons to help me, and Zimri has only himself. It's not fair that we divided the harvest equally." He went out into the night, removed a generous third of the sheaves from his harvest, and placed them with Zimri's share of the harvest.

In the meantime, Zimri sat in his home and thought, "It isn't fair that we divided the harvest equally. Abram has a wife and seven sons to feed, and I have only myself." He went out into the night, removed a generous third of the sheaves from his harvest, and placed them with Abram's share of the harvest.

The next morning the two brothers were startled to see that their harvest was the same size as it had been the day before. That night Abram again slipped out into the darkness, removed a generous third of the sheaves from his harvest, and placed them with Zimri's share. Then he crouched down in a ditch and waited. Soon he saw Zimri coming out of his home, removing a generous third of the sheaves from his harvest, and placing them with Abram's share. Abram ran from his hiding place, threw his arms around his brother, kissed him on the neck, and, being overcome with tears and emotion, was unable to speak.

In general conference many years ago, Elder Henry D. Taylor read a newspaper account that touched my heart and that reminds us all of what a difference the gift of means can make:

> The District of Columbia police auctioned off about 100 unclaimed bicycles Friday. "One dollar," said an eleven-year-old boy as the bidding opened on the first bike. The bidding, however, went much higher. "One dollar," the boy repeated hopefully each time another bike came up. The auctioneer, who had been auctioning stolen or lost bikes for 43 years, noticed that the boy's hopes seemed to soar highest whenever a racer was put up. There was one racer left. Then the bidding mounted to $8. "Sold to that boy over there for $9," said the auctioneer. He took $8 from his own pocket and asked the boy for his dollar. The youngster turned it over in small coins, took the bike, and started to leave. But he went only a few feet. Carefully parking his new possession, he went back, gratefully threw his arms around the auctioneer's neck and cried" (*Conference Report*, April 1959, 57).

The Gift of All

I recently memorized the following poem by an unknown author:

> If you know a tall fellow out ahead of a crowd
> A leader of men marching fearless and proud
> And you know a tale which the mere telling aloud
> Would cause his proud head in shame to be bowed
> It's a pretty good plan to forget it.
> If you know of a skeleton hidden away in a closet
> Guarded and kept from the day in the dark
> Whose showing, whose sudden display
> Would cause grief and sorrow and lifelong dismay
> It's a pretty good plan to forget it.

These are the kinds of gifts that are included in the *gift of all*—forgetting things in the past that could hurt another person's soul.

Many years ago I went to the hospital with Loraine Arnell, one of the elders in our ward, who had asked me to accompany him and help give a blessing to a widow in the ward. We knelt down beside her bed at Elder Arnell's instruction and prayed together; he asked me to offer the prayer. Then he asked, "Would you anoint?" When I was finished, Loraine sealed the anointing and pronounced the blessing.

As I opened my eyes, I saw tears running down Loraine's cheeks. As he bent down and kissed the woman on the cheek, I saw one of his tears drop onto her cheek. That scene touched me so much that it has become part of my own practice: whenever I give a blessing in the hospital, whether to a man, woman, or child, I kiss the person either on the forehead or the cheek—and leave there one of my own tears. Such a gift is also part of the *gift of all*.

One of our elders in the mission field, Elder Sheffield, had to undergo several surgeries before he was able to serve; his health was guarded throughout his mission, but he determined to serve with faith and dedication. One day after he returned home, I received a call from him.

"President Featherstone, I have a friend from Brazil who is dying of kidney failure," he told me. "He needs a kidney. What would you think if I gave him one of my kidneys?"

I was so overcome with emotion that I could barely answer, "You've already made up your mind, haven't you, Elder Sheffield?"

"Yes, I have," he replied. "He has a wife and two children, and I'm not married. I don't know if I'll ever get married. I've already told him that I would donate my kidney."

What a special joy filled my heart when I later learned that the kidney transplant was successful, and that Elder Sheffield's young Brazilian friend was well and whole and back with his family in a few days. Elder Sheffield—who had given the gift of all—took months to recover.

Some years ago I left a special meeting to administer to a sweet soul who was in the hospital. As I finished, I felt impressed to tell her, "I want you to know that this hand shook hands with the prophet just fifteen minutes ago." She began to softly weep.

As I held her small hand in mine, a little lady in the next bed asked, "Would you mind administering to me with that hand that shook hands with the prophet fifteen minutes ago?" Of course I responded with a blessing. Twice again the same request was repeated by the two other women who shared the hospital room. The blessings were pronounced, and all four widows in the room were consecrated. Giving of our unique talents and gifts is part of the gift of all.

Christmas will always be glorious for those who give one or more of these six precious gifts. Jesus Christ, the literal Son of God, is at the center of Christmas, and His work is not only in this world, but spans all of eternity. Through His magnificent example, He has given us these six gifts of Christmas and has set the unparalleled pattern for giving. His gifts, of course, are even greater: He has suffered exquisitely, beyond our comprehension, not only for the sinner and the wayward, but also for the orphan, the widow, the lonely, the despairing, and the heartsick. Indeed, His gifts apply to every one of us. He is the Author of peace, a peace that passeth understanding.

I pray each of us will have this peace now and always.

A QUIET PLACE CALLED BETHLEHEM

There is a quiet place on earth
    Where peace is always near,
A little town called Bethlehem,
    A place we all revere.

'Twas in the stall where Christ was born
    A manger where He laid,
Sweet Mary sang an angel's song,
    Her holy son displayed.

The shepherds and the wise men came
    To honor God's own son,
The animals and the fowls beheld
    God's gift to everyone.

Generations now have passed away
    Where heaven bent to God's great will,
The son of man, the promised one
    Would wondrous works fulfill.

Yes, Bethlehem, thou blessed town,
    A quiet place on earth;
Of all the cities great and small
    'Twas thine to house His birth.

THE LIGHT OF CHRIST IS CHRISTMAS

What is Christmas?

Christmas is reflected in the eyes of little children—not only in their excitement and anticipation, but in their tendency to draw near to the Babe in Bethlehem. It swells in their hearts—and if we listen with ears to hear, we may learn profound truths from children during the Christmas season. We are reminded of the Savior, who taught the Nephite children:

> And it came to pass that he did teach and minister unto the children of the multitude of whom hath been spoken, and he did loose their tongues, and they did speak unto their fathers great and marvelous things, even greater than he had revealed unto the people; and he loosed their tongues that they could utter (3 Nephi 26:14).

Christmas is reflected in the brightness of a singular star, set in motion to announce the birth of the Christ child. Its radiant beams still illuminate our hearts, and we wonder at the glory of its message. Its beauty and brightness stood as a sign that the weary world would no longer struggle in darkness.

Christmas is repeated in the holy strains of angels, who still sing "Glory to God in the Highest" and "Joy to the World." Imagine for a moment the singular privilege of being selected to sing in that heavenly choir! There would be no sound to rival the lyrical announcement, no hymn of the heart as beautiful as that gathering of heavenly hosts. God the Father was the choirmaster, and those who gazed into the heavens in awe would never again experience the magnificent refrain that penetrated their very soul.

The legacy for us from that wondrous heavenly choir, of course, is the selection of inspired songs we sing, bundled up in scarves and clustered against the chill under the glow of porch lights. Our minds ponder the message behind the words as we sing "Silent Night," "O Little Town of Bethlehem," "The First Noel," "The Holy City," "O Holy Night," "Still, Still, Still," and other seasonal favorites. If we listen with our spirits, we can still hear angels . . . .

The angels are not alone in reminding us, two millennia later, of that solitary scene and its eternal impact. Wise men seek Him still, journeying far to declare His divine Kingship. Do we listen to the wise? Do we craft our gifts, nestled beneath the evergreen branches, as carefully as they chose their offerings for the Christ child?

The shepherds, too, bring a remembrance of that sacred night. In reverence they bowed low and gazed on the mother and her child. They heard the stunning proclamation, listened in reverence to the heavenly hosts, and knelt in recognition of the newborn babe wrapped in swaddling clothes. Is it any wonder that this Teacher of them all would so often talk of shepherds—and that He Himself might be characterized as a dedicated shepherd who seeks us all?

He, the Master, still calls fishers of men to follow Him, leaving behind their sodden nets. He offers the spiritual equivalent of loaves and fishes to feed not only the thousands, but millions. He calms the storms and controls the elements. He feeds His flock and pastures His sheep by mending the heart and instilling peace to the soul. He lights our path and leads the way. He heals, nurtures, and satisfies the soul. All may freely come unto Him—the poor and wayfaring, the hopeless and sick, the orphan and widow, the ugly and sad, the heartsick and desperate. All who suffer can find in Him refuge from the storm.

At this Christmas season we see again the lowly stable and manger, the sweet radiance of Mary, the humble submissiveness of Joseph. We hear the choirs and proclamations. We bear testimony with Isaiah and countless other prophets. We worship and love, we live and strive, we honor and adore Him. He is the King of heaven and earth, the literal Son of God, Jesus the Christ. Oh, come, let us adore him, Christ the Lord!

UNTO THE LEAST OF THESE

'Twas the middle of the winter
    And the snow lay white and deep.
Only a few more days 'til Christmas,
    And the children sound asleep;
I went to fetch the bottle
    Where our meager savings were;
I knew it wasn't very much,
    For I'd left it up to her.
Yes, I'd left it to my darling—
    It took all that I had made
To pay the bills and buy the food,
    That's why I was afraid.
I counted out the money
    And to my wonder and surprise,
There was near a hundred dollars—
    Then tears came to my eyes.

My darling wife had managed
    To save that great amount;
She had worn her clothes all threadbare
    To make each dollar count.

I knew then that our children
    Would have a gift or two,
For they all believed in Santa Claus
    Like little children do.
My darling watched my reaction
    And she knew that I was pleased;
She said, "You know I love you,"
    Sat on my lap, and teased—
"I'll let you do the shopping
While I prepare the house,
For Christmas is a lot more fun
    When it's as tidy as a mouse."

I left her standing at the stove
    A-baking pies and bread;
I slipped into the children's room
    And kissed them all in bed.
When morning came I told my love
    "I'm going shopping, dear;
I'll take along the children,
    But don't you ever fear—
I'll not divulge their Christmas,
    I'll only watch their eyes,
And then I will remember
    To purchase their surprise."
I took my daughter Jenny,
    And my sons, Rob and Joe;
We strolled along the icy walk
    As we frolicked in the snow.

When they saw the lovely stores
    With toys of every kind,
They all got so excited
    That a gift for them I'd find.
I carefully took mental notes
    Of what they loved the best,
And I was sure I'd have enough
    To grant them their requests.
We went back home together,
    I said I had someplace to go,
I went back down to buy the gifts
    That they had wanted so.
As I bought the final toy
    And put it in my bag,
I counted out the money left,
    And my heart began to sag.

I only had a dollar left,
    With no gift for my spouse—
And I was out buying gifts
    While she cleaned up the house.
I felt my heart would break
    As it had ofttimes before.
I stood alone just wondering
    Alone there in the store.
I knew not how long it was,
    I only felt the pain.
A good man walked around me,
    Then returned to me again.

And then he up and spoke to me
    As kind as he could be—
"Sir, you have a troubled heart,
    It's not difficult to see.

"I lost my precious wife this week,
    A saint, with golden curls.
I was going to surprise her
    With this string of lovely pearls.
Perhaps you'd kindly give them
    To someone you adore,
I'd like that far better
    Than to return them to the store.
I know 'twould please my wife,
    Please share them with your love,
It would make this Christmas special
    For my someone up above."
He shook my hand so warmly,
    And wiped away a tear;
"This Christmas is a hard one,
    But now I feel her near."

I watched him walk away
    And held the pearls in my hand;
They seemed to grow in beauty,
    More lustrous on the strand.
When Christmas morning came
    And the children clapped with glee,
I watched my dearest darling
    Pull her gift from off the tree.

She carefully unwrapped it
    And to her great surprise
Lay the radiant pearl necklace.
    Then tears streamed from her eyes.
"It could not be more lovely—
    A gift fit for a queen!
I don't know how you managed it,
    For it has a golden sheen."

"But now I have a gift for you;
    I hope you like it, dear,
I slipped out while you were shopping—
    I searched most everywhere;
But nothing could I find you,
    My heart wept in despair—
I had so little money left
    I had guarded with such care.
But I did have a dollar;
    Frustrated and all alone;
I wanted so to buy a gift
    To show my love has grown.
A man came up and looked at me,
    And asked, 'Are you okay?'
I told him my dilemma;
    He brushed a tear away.

"He said, 'My darling wife has died
    Just this very week.'
Filled with so much emotion,
    He found it difficult to speak.

He reached into his pocket
    And pulled out a little box;
'She gave me this,' he whispered,
    'She was slyer than a fox.
I don't know when she bought it,
    Since she was so sick, you know;
It was her final act of love;
    Her face shone all aglow.
"Merry Christmas, beloved," she said,
    "I'll watch down over you."
Then she closed her eyes in death,
    In one last sweet adieu.

"'Life has been so good to us,
    We always joyed to give;
If you would take this little gift,
    Christ's birth for me will live.'
He almost had a holy glow
    A radiance round him shone;
One minute he was standing there,
    The next, I was alone.
So open up the box, my dear,
    It's a Christmas gift for you."
Then I carefully unwrapped it
    And held it up to view.
I stood in utter amazement—
    A gift fit for a king;
It shone in all its luster:
    A priceless ruby ring.

Its beauty beyond description!
    "It's like your string of pearls,
That were purchased for his dear wife
    To match her golden curls."
Then I recalled the other wise man
    Had a ruby and a pearl
That he had brought as his gifts
    To the King of all the world.
This truly brings the Christ child
So near this Christmas day,
For wherever this good man is,
    We think the Lord will say—
"These gifts are a memorial,
    And inasmuch as ye
Have done it unto the least of these,
Ye have done it unto Me."

THE GREATEST GIFTS OF ALL

Gifts need not be expensive in order to be deeply appreciated. In fact, as years go by, most begin to realize that the things that really matter aren't the material things at all. Most fathers and mothers in this Church would much rather have a son or daughter living the commandments, loving the Lord, being financially out of debt, knowing how to work, and having gratitude than to have a large income, a new home, a new coat, or any other more tangible gift.

The most meaningful gifts seem to involve sacrifice. Dale Harrell, one of the Scouts I served as a Scoutmaster, wrote me a letter postmarked December 14, 1979, in which he shared the following:

> Early last year, our bishop called us in to talk over our contribution to the Jordan River Temple. Together with our children, we decided that for our contribution to have any meaning to us, we must make a sacrifice. The most special and meaningful sacrifice we felt we could make was to dedicate our Christmas to the building of the Jordan River Temple. We determined how

much we usually spend on Christmas, and gave that amount to the bishop. Then each member of the family made a small gift for each other member of the family. The feeling we had was very special. I shall always treasure the memory of Christmas 1978.

Dale's touching letter reminded me of a wonderful experience our own family had with the Jordan River Temple. Just before the dedication of the temple, my wife, Merlene, had beautiful white linen handkerchiefs embroidered with the initials of each member of the family.

Two of our children were not included in the temple dedication. Paul was too young, and Lawrence was serving a mission in Scotland. During the dedication session I attended, I was seated directly behind President Spencer W. Kimball, and Merlene was seated directly behind Sister Camilla Kimball. We each had our own handkerchiefs to wave during the Hosanna Shout; in addition, I had Lawrence's handkerchief, and Merlene held Paul's handkerchief.

At last came the time during the dedication when we all stood for the Hosanna Shout, and Merlene and I prepared to each wave both of the handkerchiefs in our hands. I watched as President Kimball reached in his pocket; he withdrew his empty hand. He then searched in another pocket but was not able to find his white handkerchief. I quickly looked at the initials on the two handkerchiefs in my hand, and I gave President Kimball Lawrence's handkerchief. Imagine our joy as the prophet and president of the Church waved Lawrence's handkerchief during the Hosanna Shout, part of the dedication ceremony of the temple.

We put our missionary son's handkerchief in an envelope along with a letter and sent it to him in Scotland. When Lawrence opened the envelope, saw the white linen handkerchief with his initials embroidered in one corner, and read the letter about President Kimball waving it during the Hosanna Shout, he said he wept. That simple gift, he said, represented the greatest spiritual experience of his mission.

Gifts of value are those that represent something dear and close to our heart. No gift—not even one costing thousands of dollars—would be as precious as a note from a child committing to parents that he or she will be straight, clean, sweet, and pure. Consider the value of a simple note, an expression of love and gratitude, or a commitment to live a Christlike life.

One gift that ought to be considered during the Christmas season is the gift of music. One Christmas season I was teaching my grandchildren the fine art of "slamming" as we were sledding in one of the nearby canyons. Age caught up with me, and I broke several ribs and the second vertebra in my neck. I was unable to do much more than lie in bed during the holidays. Little did I anticipate the wonderful gift I was about to receive from my son Scott.

Scott spoke in his ward the Sunday before Christmas. Though all of our sons took piano lessons, they only endured for a year or two. Scott is our one son who broke the pain barrier and learned to play the piano well. In his talk, he told of counsel I had given him over the years: quoting Mantovani's father, I repeatedly told Scott, "Put feeling in your music, my boy." I also quoted Isaac Stern, who said, "It isn't just the notes, but the intervals between the notes, that make music beautiful." I shared every principle I had ever learned about music with Scott as he gradually honed his musical skills.

Then Scott recalled that I had asked him to memorize *Largo,* which is one of my favorite pieces of music. The lyricist entitled it *Holy Art Thou.* Once Scott had memorized the piece, he asked me to come and listen.

"My dad was impressed, and he appreciated what I had done," Scott related. "Sometime later when I was a senior in high school, I came home about midnight; I was frustrated, hurting inside, and had an aching heart. I sat down at the piano, and I suppose because I had it memorized, I began to play *Largo.* I was about halfway through the piece when I heard a noise behind me. I turned around, and there was my dad, sitting in a big easy chair with tears in his eyes. It was then that I knew I had put feeling in my music."

Feeling itself is a gift—a gift that brings us memorable moments that affect us for a lifetime. I had one of those experiences when, during the time I served in the Presiding Bishopric, I was assigned to tour the Hawaiian Mission. We made all the arrangements, prepared an itinerary, and scheduled the zone conferences and mission meetings. After reviewing the schedule, I noted to the mission president that there was no visit scheduled to Kaulapapa, the leper colony on Molokai. He explained that there were only two or three ways to reach Kaulapapa, the most reliable of which was by chartered plane. The airfield was nothing more than a strip of grass that had been cleared of other vegetation. He expressed his doubts that we would be able to reach our destination.

"I think if the Savior toured your mission, the one place he would want to go would be the leper colony," I suggested. "Please do everything in your power to see that we visit Kaulapapa."

The next day the mission president told me that he had arranged for a chartered flight. Ruth Funk and her husband, Marcus, joined us as we climbed aboard an old transport plane. We settled in the back in makeshift seats, and the door was wired closed. In less than an hour we were landing on the grass landing field.

I believe every member of the branch was there to meet us. Some wore heavy coats despite the tropical climate, just to hide the ravages of the disease. Some wore gloves. Some wore hats that partially hid their faces. We got off the plane and walked toward the people who waited for us.

The first three in line were the members of the Relief Society presidency. We reached out to shake hands with them, but they were fearful, possibly out of concern that they might spread the disease to us. We insisted, and finally, with great hesitation, these little sisters reached out their hands to us. I remember cupping their hands in mine. We shook hands with all of them. At that time I did not know whether their leprosy had been arrested; I only knew that if the Master were there, He would have embraced each sweet Saint.

Next we visited their meetinghouse; the grounds were immaculately tended, with a lush green lawn and beautiful tropical flowers and blooming shrubbery. It was easy to sense the pride these people felt in their little meetinghouse. We felt an abundance of the Spirit in that sweet, pristine little chapel where the rows of pews were separated by a wide aisle. Jack Sing, the branch president, explained that one side was for those with leprosy, and the other was for those who did not have the disease. President Sing couldn't remember exactly how long he had been branch president, but he knew it was longer than twenty years. He explained that he could have left the island years earlier, since his leprosy had been arrested, but he chose to stay in the leper colony with his faithful wife.

During our tour of the island, we saw the cemetery where members of the Church had been buried. Most of the cemetery was overrun with vegetation, but the LDS section was trimmed, mowed, and given special care.

When we finished our visit, we returned to the grass airfield. I believe every member of the branch was there to see us off. They waved as we taxied down the grassy runway. As we lifted into the air, I thought, "I walked today where Jesus walked." The gift of that visit filled my heart and created in me something very close to the Christmas spirit.

If we will but recognize them as such, we will find that there are many experiences that fill our souls with the Christmas spirit and that bring us the gifts of greatest value. I remember the story of a ragged old tramp knocking at the back door of a home one morning and asking for something to eat. He was invited in to the kitchen to rest while a meal was prepared for him. Drink had driven him deep into sin, and he was convinced that no one cared for him.

A little boy sat near the table and watched the man with curiosity. Finally the little boy walked over to the old man, laid his hand on his coat sleeve, and looked up into his face. "Man, does you love Dod?" he asked. When the old tramp did not reply, the little boy said, "Well, man, Dod loves you."

The tramp's eyes filled with tears, and his hands trembled. The little fellow then ran to his room and returned with ten pennies; he pressed them into the old man's hand as he said, "Man, this will buy you something." The old tramp bowed his head and shed tears over years of silent suffering. He stood and left the house without saying a word.

Months later, the little boy received a letter. In its simple lines were penned the sentiments, "Little one, you saved me from hell. For days all I could hear was, 'Man, Dod loves you.'

Finally I remembered what I used to be and cried out, 'Oh, God, if it isn't too late, make me a child once more, and let me see that little child in heaven, if not down here.' I've now got a job, clothes, and a place to sleep. I'm an old man and won't be here long, but God bless you, child, because you led an old dirty tramp back to God." Sometimes the greatest gift can be the simplest words of a child.

President Joseph F. Smith shared a memorable Christmas in the January 1919 issue of the *Improvement Era,* in which he realized the choicest gifts in his life:

> There were our precious chicks, but not a dollar in cash, with which to buy one thing for Christmas. I could draw a few pounds of flour, or meat, a little molasses, or something of that kind, ahead, at the general tithing office and pay up at the end of that month with tithing scrip, received in payment of my labor which more often than not began at 6 a.m. and ended at 11 p.m. at $3 per day in tithing pay, which was not cash.
>
> I saw many reveling in luxuries, with means to lavish on their every want, which were far more than their needs—riding in buggies, on prancing horses, enjoying their leisure, while we all were on foot and of necessity tugging away with all our might to keep soul and body together. Under these spiritless conditions, one day just before Christmas, I left the old home with feelings I cannot describe. I wanted to do something for my chicks. I wanted something to

please them and to mark the Christmas day from all other days—but not a cent to do it with! I walked up and down Main Street, looking into the shop windows—into Amussen's jewelry store, to every store—everywhere—and then slunk out of sight of humanity and sat down and wept like a child, until my poured-out grief relieved my aching heart; and after awhile returned home, as empty as when I left, and played with my children, grateful and happy only for them and their beloved mother.

Sometimes the gifts closest to our hearts are spoken in a few simple words. Years ago I was invited to speak at a BYU devotional to approximately 18,000 students; it was a humbling assignment, and I spent weeks preparing for it. Elder Dallin H. Oaks, then the president of BYU, sat on the stand next to me and my wife. During my talk, I told the students I wanted to share a thought with them—and that, since my wife was on the stand, I also wanted to share a thought with her.

In the movie *Camelot,* King Arthur learns that Guinevere has been unfaithful to him with Sir Lancelot; the two people King Arthur loved most on the earth had betrayed him together. He locked himself in a lonely chamber with a high vaulted ceiling and expressed the thoughts of his heart. I told the students that King Arthur's expressions very nearly echoed my own:

> Proposition: If I could choose, from every woman who breathes on this earth, the face I would most love, the breath, the smile, the touch, the voice, the heart, the laugh, the soul itself, every detail

and feature to the smallest strand of hair—they would all be Jenny's.

That, I told the crowd of students assembled, was how I felt about my own sweet wife, Merlene.

Two weeks later we were watching a BYU devotional on television, and they announced that the speaker would be Vaughn Featherstone. I said, "Merlene, come over here, and watch this with me." It is really humbling to watch yourself on television.

When it got to the King Arthur quote in my talk and I said, "This is how I feel about my wife," the camera man focused on Merlene, and her face filled the television screen. As I began the words, "Proposition: If I could choose. . . ." her tears flowed freely. She was deeply touched. I became emotional when I saw how much it affected her. I couldn't even look at her for a few minutes until that part of my talk was over, and I gained some composure. I slid over close to her; again the tears flowed freely. Just hearing it again on television touched her deeply.

Sometime after that I visited the Bloomfield Hills Michigan Stake and toured the Montreal Canada Mission. I concluded the weekend by conducting a stake conference in Caldwell, New Jersey. About 10:30 Sunday night I drove up the street where we live. I was exhausted and fatigued beyond belief.

A bishop who had served in our ward almost thirty years ago said, "Whenever you go home, always go home happy. Don't take your problems or work home with you. Be happy." He suggested that we would relieve the burden in a heavy heart if we would follow this simple advice. To this day, every time I drive up our street, I remember Bishop Paul Pehrson's words . . . "Always go home happy. . . ."

But that late Sunday night, I thought to myself, "I don't *feel* happy." Then I told myself, "You've got to do it; you have been away for a long time." I got out of the car, took a couple of deep breaths, picked up both suitcases, walked to the door, pushed it open, and called out with a cheery voice—despite my bone-weary exhaustion—"Hi, I'm home!"

Jill ran up and hugged me. Each of the boys came running. I hugged and loved each one. Then I went to the bottom of the stairs and looked up at my wife, who was standing on the top step. I smiled at her and said, "Hi, sweetheart, I'm home."

"I know," she said, "but you forgot what day it is, didn't you?"

"No, I didn't forget," I smiled. Then I dropped my head and thought hard. Suddenly it dawned on me: it was our anniversary, and I *had* forgotten. I didn't tell her that. As she came down the stairs, three distinct ideas came to my mind. First, I tried to remember if someone had given me something that I could give to her, saying it was from me. They had not. Second, I realized it was Sunday, and knew I couldn't go shopping. A man doesn't care if he gets a gift a week early or a week late, but a woman needs her gift during that twenty-four-hour period. Before she got to the bottom step I had my third thought: "Write her a check." Well, a check is not that impressive.

I hugged her without admitting that I had forgotten our anniversary. I talked with the family for a few minutes and shared some spiritual experiences with them; then I hugged the children, kissed them, and sent them to bed. I put my arm around my wife's waist, and we walked upstairs together. Not a word was spoken.

I felt terrible. I wasn't tired or exhausted—I hurt inside for this great woman who never complains and is always supportive.

We changed and knelt down by the bed. I offered a prayer, then kissed my wife and told her I loved her. She climbed into bed, and I went around on my side and climbed in beside her. I remember lying on my back with my hands behind my head, thinking about my wife. A shaft of light from outside shone on the ceiling. I stared at it for about five minutes. I remember thinking, "Heavenly Father, you knew it was our anniversary. It wouldn't have hurt to have a little help. I was on a Church assignment." Then I repented from that and lay there thinking about this marvelous, uncomplaining woman that I was sure was hurt but wouldn't say anything. I knew she was probably staring at the same light on the ceiling. Finally, I broke the silence.

"Merlene?"

"What?"

"I guess you know I forgot."

"I know," she responded; the hurt in her voice was obvious.

I turned to face her. "I don't know what to say to you except this. Proposition: If I could choose from every woman who breathes on this earth, the face I would most love, the smile, the touch, the voice, the heart, the laugh, the soul itself, every detail and feature to the smallest strand of hair—they would all be yours."

She let me off the hook with that—but, then, she knows that is exactly how I feel about her. She is the most Christlike, considerate, feeling woman, a person with a buoyant spirit who loves openly and freely. That is her gift to me, just as my expression of love was my gift to her.

At this Christmas season, I hope that our Father will bless all those who have lost their spouses through death or divorce—those homes where half of the bed is cold where once it was warm.

I pray that He will bless those good parents whose children have strayed, causing a heartache that has yet to be relieved.

I pray that He might bless the poor who are honest, who have pride, who are independent, and who suffer in silence.

I pray that He will bless those who are ill or who have loved ones who are ill, even though no one ever knows.

I pray that He will bless those who "sleep not" because their hearts are too heavy—those who are burdened with debt, who never seem to make it, who have no friends to turn to . . . those who are lonely and who feel that no one cares.

I pray that God will bless us all and make His face to shine upon us, His love to enshroud us, and His care to ever tend us.

These, and more, are His precious gifts to us. If the Lord God Jehovah can place billions of stars in the cosmos, he can certainly cause one star to hang in suspended brilliance over Bethlehem, testifying that Jesus Christ is the literal, physical Son of God.

The Savior of all mankind has not only given the gifts mentioned and set the unparalleled pattern for giving, but He has given more. He has suffered exquisitely beyond comprehension, not only for the sinner and the wayward but also for the orphan, the widow, the lonely, the despairing, the heavy-hearted. No soul who walks this earth will ever suffer through any experience that He has not felt nor endured vicariously.

President Howard W. Hunter said:

> The real Christmas comes to him who has taken Christ into his life as a moving, dynamic, vitalizing force. The real spirit of Christmas lies in the life and mission of the Master. . . .

> If you desire to find the true spirit of Christmas and partake of the sweetness of it, let me make this suggestion to you. During the hurry of the festive occasion of this Christmas season, find time to turn your heart to God. Perhaps in the quiet hours, and in a quiet place, and on your knees—alone or with loved ones—give thanks for the good things that have come to you, and ask that his spirit might dwell in you as you earnestly strive to serve him and keep his commandments. He will take you by the hand and his promises will be kept. ("The Real Christmas," in *Speeches of the Year, 1972-1973* [Provo, Utah: Brigham Young University Press, 1973, 67-69).

His gift to mankind is magnificent beyond description. His life is singular without comparison. His love and compassion reach beyond the eternities. Let us all—rich and poor, homely and beautiful, happy and sad, lonely and heartsick—turn to Him. The best things in life really are from God.

Helen Steiner Rice wrote a poem adapted from an old German legend that underscores the importance of our focus at Christmas:

The Story of the Christmas Guest

It happened one day at the year's white end,
   Two neighbors called on an old-time friend
And they found his shop meager and mean,
   Made gay with a thousand boughs of green,
And Conrad was sitting with face a-shine

When he suddenly stopped as he stitched a twine
And said, "Old friends, at dawn today,
When the cock was crowing the night away
The Lord appeared in a dream to me
And said, "I am coming your guest to be" . . .
So I've been busy with feet astir,
Strewing my shop with branches of fir,
The table is spread and the kettle is shined
And over the rafters the holly is twined,
And now I will wait for my Lord to appear
And listen closely so I will hear
His step as He nears my humble place,
And I open the door and look in His face. . . ."

So his friends went home and left Conrad alone,
For this was the happiest day he had known,
For, long since, his family had passed away
And Conrad has spent a sad Christmas day . . .
But he knew with the Lord as his Christmas guest
This Christmas would be the dearest and best,
And he listened with only joy in his heart.
And with every sound he would rise with a start
And look for the Lord to be standing there
In answer to his earnest prayer . . .
So he ran to the window after hearing a sound,
But all that he saw on the snow-covered ground
Was a shabby beggar whose shoes were torn
And all of his clothes were ragged and worn . . .
So Conrad was touched and went to the door
And he said, "Your feet must be frozen and sore,

And I have some shoes in my shop for you
   And a coat that will keep you warmer, too."
So with grateful heart the man went away,
   But as Conrad noticed the time of day
He wondered what made the dear Lord so late
   And how much longer he'd have to wait,
When he heard a knock and ran to the door,
   But it was only a stranger once more,
A bent, old crone with a shawl of black,
   A bundle of faggots piled on her back,
She asked for only a place to rest,
   But that was reserved for Conrad's Great Guest . . .
But her voice seemed to plead, "Don't send me away,
   Let me rest for awhile on Christmas Day."

So Conrad brewed her a steaming cup
   And told her to sit at the table and sup . . .
But after she left he was filled with dismay
   For he saw that the hours were passing away
And the Lord had not come as He said He would,
   And Conrad felt sure he had misunderstood. . .
When out of the stillness he heard a cry,
   "Please help and tell me where am I."
So again he opened his friendly door
   And stood disappointed as twice before,
It was only a child who had wandered away
   And was lost from her family on Christmas Day. . . .

Again Conrad's heart was heavy and sad,
   But he knew he should make this little child glad,

So he called her in and wiped her tears
    And quieted her childish fears . . .
Then he led her back to her home once more
But as he entered his own darkened door,
He knew that the Lord was not coming today
    For the hours of Christmas had passed away . . .
So he went to his room and knelt down to pray
    And he said, "Dear Lord, why did you delay,
What kept you from coming to call on me,
    For I wanted so much your face to see . . . "
When soft in the silence a voice he heard,
    "Lift up your head, for I kept my word . . .
Three times my shadow crossed your floor . . .
    Three times I came to your lonely door . . .
For I was the beggar with bruised, cold feet,
    I was the woman you gave to eat,
And I was the child on the homeless street."

This Christmas, let us give gifts that will enlarge and magnify the gifts from Christ. Let us not search for material things, but for the things of God. I promise you peace will come, hope will increase, and rewards for eternity will be yours. Reach out at this Christmas season with gifts of self—love, time, and service. You will have, and give, the merriest of all Christmases by giving the gifts of God.

A CHRISTMAS HYMN

The Lamb of God, Most Holy, is loved this Christmas day,
    And men and angels worship Him in what they do and say.
Women and children adore Him and sing carols to His name,
    While the great and noble of the earth are shadowed in His fame.

This glorious Jesus blessed the sick, healed the deaf, the blind and lame,
    And weary, heartsick, tired folks in pleading call His name.
For in His life they find the hope, that none but He can give.
    His living love is charity; He taught us how to live.

What will we do who know His work and understand His care?
    When will we watch with eager eyes, His gospel love to share?
Where will we find Him in our quest to gain eternal realms?
    The infant babe, the Nazarene, the Christ of Heaven's realms.

THE LIGHT OF HOPE

In 1979 Lowell Durham, then the president of Deseret Book Company, came to my office. He explained that each year the company liked to publish a little Christmas booklet that wards might consider giving as gifts for Christmas. He told me that President Spencer W. Kimball had written the first booklet. The next year, they had invited President Thomas S. Monson to write the second booklet. Now, sitting across from my desk, Lowell wondered how I would feel about writing the third booklet.

I don't know when I have been so excited over an assignment!

Before I could enjoy my excitement too much, Lowell said, "We hate to do this to you, but we can only give you six weeks to finish the booklet. I have hope that six weeks will be sufficient time."

That night I couldn't sleep. I had ideas darting through my head and a two-inch-thick folder full of Christmas ideas at my office. Finally, unable to quiet my mind, I got up at 2:00 a.m. and made my way through the still darkness to the Church Office Building. I grabbed my file, looked through all the ideas I had collected over the years, and went to work.

I wrote in a notebook for the next six hours.

When my secretary arrived at work, I handed her my first draft, and she typed it for me. Two hours later she gave me a beautiful typewritten copy of the first draft. I quickly edited it, and she retyped it.

Just before 11:00 that morning, I called Lowell Durham and announced that I had the draft for the Christmas booklet. I am confident he silently worried about the quality of that manuscript!

Lowell picked up the manuscript, read it, reduced it by about a third, and approved it to be published.

What no one at Deseret Book realized is how amazing I felt at the wonderful challenge to write a booklet about Christmas—about what it means to me—and how privileged I felt to be able to honor the Savior of the world in such a unique way. It was a supreme motivator! My brain was exhilarated and my heart was filled with the Spirit—which seemed to set my pen on fire.

What follows is the Christmas message from *The Light of Hope,* the booklet I wrote through a dark, still night in an effort to bring some light to a dark, still world. It was humbling to write, and every time I read it, I reflect on the wonderful opportunity to draw closer to Christ at Christmas. I hope it brings Christ's Spirit into your Christmas.

The Light of Hope

We receive great blessings because others share. I do not refer to gifts, as appreciated as they are. I refer to the sacred, soul-moving experiences others have had that enlarge our souls and strip away false pride.

Christmas is a time to humble ourselves by focusing on things of true worth. It is a time of peace and goodwill toward all men. It is a time of mercy and understanding. It is a time to put Jesus in His proper place in our lives. The principles of His gospel practiced in daily lives produce the most heart-touching and meaningful feelings.

Many years ago I recall hearing President Harold B. Lee tell a story of a family from Montpelier, Idaho. He referred to them as the Brown family, although that was not their real name. The husband was off in a distant city trying to support the family, but he was actually able to do little more than support himself. His board and room took up most of his income and left precious little to send home to his family.

The little family survived as best they could. One evening, as the mother and the five children sat down at the dinner table, all the food in the house was placed in front of them—a quart of milk. She poured the milk into five glasses and reminded the children that this was all the food they had. Then she suggested that the one saying the blessing ask the Lord to please bless them with food. This was done. After the blessing the oldest son reminded his mother that she had not poured any milk for herself. She quickly responded that she had had some earlier. The children drank their milk and then went into the parlor.

Later that evening Sister Brown was sitting in the rocking chair, gently rocking, with the children gathered around her on the floor. She told them of their dire circumstances and said, "Let us kneel together and ask Heavenly Father to please bless us that we will have food." Then she knelt with her children in front of the rocking chair and prayed for her family and her husband, and for food. As they arose from their knees, she hugged and kissed each one and sent them upstairs to bed. When she came to the oldest son, she could see great concern in his eyes and a heavy expression on his face. She held him close and said, "Son, we have just been talking to the Lord. Now don't you worry—He will provide food for the family. Everything is going to be all right." The youth went upstairs, tucked each of the children in, and then climbed into bed. However, sleep would not come. He lay in bed and worried about food for his family. As the oldest son, he filled the role of the "man of the family" while the father was away. He stared at the ceiling for what seemed hours; then he heard a noise downstairs. He quietly got out of bed, crept over to the stairs, and went partway down. His mother was kneeling in front of the rocking chair praying. He heard the words, "Please, Heavenly Father, we don't have any food. I promised my children we would have food. Please don't let them lose faith."

The stairs squeaked, and the mother looked up from her prayer and saw her son. He impulsively ran downstairs and threw his arms around her. She hugged him with one arm and wiped the tears from her face with the other hand. Then she held his face in both hands, looked into his eyes, and said again, "Don't worry, son. I have just been talking to the Lord, and everything is going to be just fine." Once again she kissed him and sent him upstairs to bed. And again he lay awake for a long time. Finally he trailed off into a deep sleep. The next thing he could recollect is that he was awakened by the aroma of food being cooked. He awakened the other children and they ran downstairs to the kitchen. The table and cupboards and counters were loaded with groceries: salt pork, eggs, flour, potatoes, milk, meat, and vegetables. The oldest son said, "Mother where did all this food come from?" She replied, "Never you mind, son. I told you that the Lord would provide, and He has."

Many years later, when the son had grown tall, moved to Arizona, and been called as a stake president, his mother died. He returned to Montpelier for the funeral. After the funeral the elderly stake patriarch spoke to him. "Do you remember when your family was out of food?"

"I remember!"

"Did you ever learn where the food came from?" He responded that he did not.

Then the patriarch said, "You know, I was bishop at that time. I came home late one night exhausted, and my wife told me to go sit down in the parlor and read the paper while she prepared supper. As I sat down and started to read, a voice said to me, 'Sister Brown needs food.' I called to my wife and asked her what she had said. She said, 'I didn't say anything. What did you hear?' 'I heard a voice say that Sister Brown needs food.' Then my wife said to me, 'I guess you'd better hitch the horses to the wagon and go over to the storehouse and get some food for Sister Brown.' I went over to the storehouse and loaded the wagon with food and dropped it by your house at a very late hour."

This wonderful story is one that I tell quite often, because it reminds us that the Lord answers prayers through his servants who love Him and love their fellowmen.

Many of the noble acts of life are done by those we would least suspect. Elder Randy Lowry, a missionary in the Texas San Antonio Mission, told us of a little boy who went to his mother's closet and took out her dress shoes, which were caked with dried mud and dirt from a recent storm. He washed the shoes and waxed and polished them. Then he waxed and polished them a second time; and finally, when they looked like new, he took them to his mother. She could hardly believe her eyes. She hugged him, kissed him—and went to her purse and took out a quarter, which she dropped into his hand. He looked at her with a deeply puzzled expression, put the quarter in his pocket, and returned the beautifully waxed and polished shoes to her closet. Several hours later the mother went to change her clothes to go to the store. As she put on the freshly cleaned and shined shoes, she felt something in the toe of one of them. She took the shoe off and shook it. A piece of paper fell into her upturned palm. As she opened the paper, a quarter fell to the floor. Then she read these words: "Mother, I did it for love."

Christmas is a time that reminds us that we do things for love. Love is charity, and charity is the pure love of Christ, "which never faileth."

About three or four years ago I had the privilege of attending a national Boy Scouts of America meeting in the eastern United States. Elder Thomas S. Monson, who serves on the national board of the Boy Scouts of America, also attended the meeting. He invited me to his hotel room for a discussion, and we talked for two or three hours.

It seemed as if the hotel room had been changed into a sacred temple room because of his great spirit.

Toward the close of our discussion, he reminisced about his experiences as a young bishop, called at the age of twenty-two. He said there were eighty-seven widows in his ward. Each year while he was a bishop he visited each one at Christmas and gave her a food basket or special gift. After his release he continued to visit each widow every Christmas. While he served as mission president, he had someone else visit them for him and take each one a large roasting chicken or a box of candy. Then I remember what a sweet spirit swept over me as he tenderly said, "I still visit them, but there are only a few left." He knew exactly how many there were and kept track from year to year. I believe that is what an Apostle of the Lord Jesus Christ would do, and I knew he would do it for love. I believe it is what Jesus would do.

A mother's love comes closest to the measure of the love of Christ. Thank God for the wonderful mothers who have always made Christmas so special. Mother is the one who urges the early purchase of the Christmas tree. She brings her daily addition to the Christmas decorations in the home. She it is who carefully decides which gifts would be most special. My own sweet mother, who has never really had very much for herself, buys a Christmas gift for every child, grandchild, and great-grandchild, often at great sacrifice on her part. We have lovingly counseled her not to try to buy everyone a gift, but she insists. How wonderful is her sweet spirit! How foolish we are to try to stop the flow of goodness from our noble mother!

John Wesley gave us a formula for a saintly life. Christmastime may bring us the few moments when we look to evaluate our virtues. In the simplest words he said:

> Do all the good you can,
> By all the means you can,
> In all the ways you can,
> In all the places you can,
> At all the times you can,
> To all the people you can,
> As long as ever you can.

That is it. That is what the Christmas spirit should help us all resolve to do. The men who come nearest to this model are the prophets and Apostles, especially our beloved prophet. What strength and blessing he has brought to the Church!

Some time ago I presided over the Texas San Antonio Mission. While we were there a tragic accident occurred. On the day of stake conference, Brother Rockwood, a true Latter-day Saint, was on his way to a meeting when another car crossed into the wrong lane and he was killed in the accident. Sister Rockwood, a great mother, a seminary teacher, and an outstanding woman, was critically injured. She has since recovered to raise her seven children alone. At Christmas time we received a Christmas letter from the family. At the top of the letter was this simple heading: "Our Christmas Letter and a Tribute to Dad." This is their tribute:

> If we could have chosen a time or a season for him to leave us, it would never have been in the springtime, because we always plant our rosebushes and flower beds . . . and he tills the garden . . . and we take drives to see the wild flowers . . . and the trees blossom and bud.
>
> We become so excited about spring and trips and fun . . . times and there is Joe's birthday, and our anniversary . . . and walks on the riverwalk on Friday night. No, we could never endure the spring without his happy smile, sparkling eyes, and all our new plans.
>
> And it couldn't be in summer when he leaves us, because he is going to teach the boys to swim, and

cook the hamburgers on the grill, and take us for a weekend on the coast. He has to be here for July 4 . . . his birthday is the 5th, and we celebrate them together. And how could he not be here for Chris's and Carter's birthdays . . . and eating homemade ice cream off the paddle? No, summer would not be the right time.

But then, how about autumn? How can little boys come rushing home with excitement over their new teacher, and a daughter start college, and a married daughter give him a new granddaughter—if he's not here? And Linda must have her birthday. No, autumn has too much excitement . . . too many new starts. Whom would I share my seminary lessons with? And besides, in the fall sometimes the evenings are chilly, and we may need a fire in the fireplace. . ..

Winter for sure would bring chilly nights and toes to be warmed. . . and all the happy holidays . . . and Kathi's and Kelli's birthdays. He must be here to crack the pecans for pecan pie. And how can we make chocolate chip cookies without his "snatches" from the dough? We would have such a hard time singing loud enough when we go caroling, with his voice missing. And he always plays Santa and reads the Christmas story from Luke and Third Nephi on Christmas Eve. New Year's Day is the time we set our yearly goals and review last year's accomplishments. He presides at this family council—and we need him to be here. No, winter isn't right . . . far too many special occasions and too many goals to set. But that brings us back to spring. . ..

He did leave us in the spring. . . with a garden only started, and our anniversary just celebrated that very day. He had appointments in his book that were important and needed to be kept. He had personal interviews with the children scheduled through May . . . and rosebushes still to plant . . . and we wondered how we could endure. But then we remembered a family in white around an altar, and recalled the words "For time and all eternity," and we were strengthened. We are promised that if we are faithful, someday soon all the eternal things of this life will be ours . . . together. Someday we will never have to part.

His leaving seems to say to each of us, "Don't become so concerned with the cares of this life that the spirit is neglected. This life is but a moment, and it will be only those things of the spirit that we have nurtured that will go with us."

Among Phil's possessions we found this quotation handwritten on an index card: "Peace comes to a man when he loves his wife as himself, honors her more than himself, leads his children in the right path and looks to their welfare when he is with them or not."

May we add, peace has also come to his family.

> We send you all our love this Christmas season and express our appreciation for the life and sacrifice of Jesus Christ. We bear you our solemn witness that He lives, and because He lives, we all shall live again.

This sweet little family has found the Christ in Christmas. Their perspective has lengthened from the day to day and year to year to all eternity. The physical gifts of toy, clothes, and sports equipment fade into obscurity, and the true gifts of the Master have rested in their souls.

When I was called to be a stake president, I made a decision that not one member family residing in our very large stake would not have a Christmas. We had personal priesthood interviews with all the bishops and asked them to see that every family had a turkey on the table for Christmas, and food and other gifts for family members. I checked personally with every bishop the Sunday preceding Christmas. Every needy family had been identified, a sub for Santa had been provided, turkeys and food baskets had been purchased and prepared for delivery.

One Sunday evening that Christmas season I spoke at the Eagle Ward sacrament meeting. My heart was full, for I knew the Master would be pleased with the wonderful work of our bishops. I addressed my remarks to the thirteenth chapter of First Corinthians, Paul's great discourse on charity. At the conclusion of my talk I said, "I think the Savior would be pleased with the wonderful things that are being done by our bishops and others who are seeing that every family in this stake has a turkey on the table for Christmas dinner and food and gifts for the family." I restrained as best I could the tears that were coming. Then I sat down, and we sang a lovely carol in honor of the Savior and Master.

As the meeting ended, I shook hands with many ward members. Suddenly I was faced by a young boy about nine or ten years of age. He reminded me of myself at that age. He had on a white T-shirt, Levis, and logger boots. He looked up at me and said, "Good speech, mister." I said, "Thanks, son. Are you going to have a turkey dinner and gifts for Christmas?" He said, "No, sir. My dad is out of work, and he said you have to pay Santa Claus for all gifts." He then continued, "We have saved a deer roast that Mom will cook for Christmas dinner, but we won't have that turkey you talked about, and we won't have any gifts." I put my arm around him and walked down the aisle of the chapel. I would not have felt any closer to the Savior if He had been walking where the boy was. I took him to the bishop and said, "Bishop, this young man said that his family is not going to have a turkey dinner. They can't pay Santa Claus for their gifts, so they are not going to have a Christmas—at least that's what he tells me."

The bishop looked at the boy with puzzlement. I am sure he was trying to tie him to a family in the ward. Suddenly his eyes lighted up. "You are the _____ boy," he said. The boy nodded yes. Then the bishop said to me, "Don't worry, President. We hadn't remembered this family, but they will have a Christmas, and they will have a turkey on the table." He put his arm around the boy, and they went into the bishop's office to talk.

This magnificent church is His church. He will not leave his leaders without constant guidance and direction for the welfare of His people. He will also respond to each one of us. We are His, and He will bless us during our darkest hours. He will bring His "peace on earth" to the heart of everyone who will come unto Him.

We, then, must look to our gifts to others. Indeed, is not the servant greatest? At this special Christmas hour, we—all of God's children—have greatest cause to rejoice. We have found the Messiah; we know the great "I Am." We have found our King of kings, our Lord of lords. We adore His holy name. We love Him.

Let us resolve as Saints in His church that we will carry the Christmas spirit year 'round. Of all the people on the earth, He looks to us, His little flock, to bless the world—a world that celebrates a pagan holiday, and gives and shares with selfish motives; a world that has office parties where sin and licentiousness are the norm; a world where the poor are ground into the earth; a world that has forsaken Him and His teachings.

How refreshing it must be that His people—each one of us in His church, who know that He was not born on December 25 but on April 6—should take this time to make Christmas a holy day of adoration, worship, and service. Oh, how we ought to thank our beloved Father in Heaven for the gift of His Son!

Ida Norton Minson affirms that Christ still walks beside mankind on the way:

Twilight. And on a dusty ribboned way,
Out from Jerusalem, two travelers walked.

Gray shadows touched their feet, but deeper lay
The shadows in their hearts. They softly talked
Of days just passed, of hopeless days in view,
Of boats, of nets, the while their eyes were dim;
Of Galilee, the work they used to do,
Their voices often stilled, remembering Him.
A stranger also walked that way, and when
They sensed his nearness, some new sympathy
Assuaged their grief. Old hopes came warm again
As, in the dusk, he kept them company. . . .
Thus, through the troubled twilight of today
Emmaus road has stretched its shining thread
And still Christ walks beside men on the way,
To hold the light of hope, to break the bread.

May we hold the light of hope and walk with Him—not just at this season, but also in the springtime, in summer, in autumn, and in winter. Let us give the gifts of service to all we meet, the gifts that will bring peace and love and harmony to the world.

SOME OF THEM DO SPARKLE

As you will recall from the movie *Camelot*, Mordred, the king's illegitimate son, moves in to accelerate the ruin of the Round Table. Guenevere is to be burned at the stake, but Lancelot saves her during a daring rescue. Finally, just before the misty dawn on a quiet battlefield in France, Arthur is alone behind the lines when Lancelot brings Guenevere to King Arthur.

It's a solemn scene. Repair is impossible. Battle is inevitable. And, perhaps saddest of all for Arthur, his dream of Camelot is about to end. Because of his great love for both Guenevere and Lancelot, he forgives them; they leave, and he is once more left alone on a still and silent battlefield.

Suddenly, he hears a faint rustling sound in the nearby brush.

"Who's there?" demands Arthur. "Who is out there? Come out, I say."

Slowly, an earnest-looking boy emerges from the brush; he stands at attention and answers, "Forgive me, Your Majesty. I was searching for the sergeant of arms, and I got lost. I did not wish to disturb you."

"Who are you?" Arthur asks. "Where did you come from?" Then, noticing the boy's tender age, he queries, "Are you a page? You ought to be in bed!"

The boy quickly squares up his shoulders and replies, "Forgive me, Your Majesty, but I came to fight for the Round Table! I'm very good with a bow," he explains, exuding confidence. "I will kill the enemy."

Arthur struggles to keep from laughing at the boy who believes himself to be stronger than the enemy troops. "But what if they kill you?" he challenges.

Undeterred, the boy answers, "Then I will be dead, miLord, but I don't intend to be killed. I intend to be a knight."

Arthur rubs his chin and looks into the boy's eyes. "A knight?"

"Yes, miLord," the boy responds, stretching to his full stature and sticking out his chest, "a knight of the Round Table."

"Oh," Arthur nods. "And when did you decide on this extinct profession? Was your welfare protected by knights? Was your father a knight? Or was your mother saved by one?"

"Oh, no, miLord," the boy replies with great seriousness. "I had never seen a knight until I stowed away. I only know them by the stories people tell."

Arthur is visibly moved by the boy's explanation. "From the stories people tell, you wish to become a knight?" he asks, quietly. "Now, tell me what you think you know of the Knights of the Round Table."

The boy draws closer to Arthur. "I know everything, miLord. Might for right, right for right, justice for all. A round table where all knights would sit. Everything!"

Arthur beckons the boy to come closer. "What is your name?"

"Tom of Warwick, Sir."

Arthur looks into the boy's eyes; there is quiet resolve in his voice. "You will not fight, Tom," he tells him. "You will run behind the lines and live to return to England. You will do everything I, the King, tell you. Each evening from December to December, before you drift to sleep upon your cot, think back on all the tales that you remember of Camelot. Ask every person if he has heard the story, and tell it strong and loud and clear if he has not. Camelot! Now, say it loud and with great joy. Camelot! Yes, come, my boy. Don't let it be forgot, that once there was a spot, for one brief, shining moment, that was known as Camelot!"

Arthur's friend, Pellinore, approaches to announce that it is time to prepare for battle.

"Pellinore, give me your sword," Arthur says. He motions for Tom to kneel before him. "With this sword, Excalibur, I knight thee, Sir Tom of Warwick. I command you to return home and carry out my orders."

Astonished, Tom rises to his feet, and a smile spreads across his face. "Yes, miLord!" he cries as he runs off into the brush, his blond hair barely visible as he runs into the distance.

"Return home!" Arthur cries after him. "Run behind the lines! Run, Tom!"

Pellinore gazes at Arthur in confusion. "Who was that boy?"

"One of what we all are, Pelli," Arthur replies quietly. "Less than a drop of the great blue emotion of this unlit sea, but it seems that some of the drops sparkle. Some of them do sparkle, Pelli." Then, crying out with all his strength, he shouts into the still morning air, "Run, boy! Oh, run, my boy!"

In my lifetime, I have been privileged to see some of those who sparkle. We taught Charles Dye of Lexington, Kentucky, the missionary discussions against his parents' will. They were opposed to his baptism. After he joined the Church, his parents demanded that he either abandon the Church or move out. If he stayed in the Church and chose instead to move out, they warned him, he would never see them—or his three brothers and sisters—again.

He confessed with powerful emotion how much he loved his parents. He shared with us the inner feelings he struggled with when he considered never seeing them again. He thought his heart would break. Then he resolutely stated, "But I know the gospel is true, and I had to follow the Master." Oh, how some of them do sparkle.

John Barrett, a good friend of mine, moved from Austin, Texas, to Manti, Utah; a wonderful, Christlike man, he is now almost completely blind. Though he is skilled and has worked hard all his life, his failed eyesight makes it very difficult for him to find work. His resources have been completely exhausted.

At one point, John needed a car. A man in the ward was selling a van for $600; the van didn't run and needed repairs that would require additional investment above and beyond the asking price of $600. John, still unable to find a job, didn't have the $600, but he patiently waited. Several months passed, and the van remained unsold. Finally John approached the owner and said, "I would like to buy your van for $300."

The owner thought it over, then said, "Well, it's just sitting here—and I guess $300 is better than nothing." John handed over the $300, and the van was his.

John tried to work on the van and made what repairs he could, but he did not have money to buy the necessary parts. Several more months passed, and John found himself in desperate financial straits. Finally, with some reluctance, he let it be known that the van was for sale.

Another member of the ward approached John and asked, "How much do you want for your van?"

John said that he would be grateful to get at his $300 back.

The good brother smiled and said, "You say you want $300?"

"That would be great," John responded.

The man then rubbed his chin, paused a moment, and asked, "All right, will you take $400?"

"That would be wonderful!" John replied.

The brother then asked, "Well, then, will you take $500 for it?"

Puzzled, John didn't know *what* to say. But that wasn't the end of it. Finally, this kind and good Saint said, "This is my final offer. Would you take $600 for the van?"

It was easy to see John's desperate need as the tears flowed in response to such a sweet experience. Oh, how some of them *do* sparkle.

A sweet couple came to my office one day; the pregnant wife had been counseled by her physicians to have an abortion because of serious defects that appeared to plague her developing baby. The lines of worry were etched deeply as she and her husband voiced their concern.

We counseled together, and then I gave her a blessing. In the blessing she was promised a miracle. She was told that God can do all things, and that it being His holy will, He could surely heal the expected baby boy.

Rallying their faith, this wonderful couple followed the counsel in the blessing—trusting in the Lord—instead of submitting to an abortion, which would have meant putting their trust in the arm of flesh. Several months after his Christmas-season birth, I received two pictures of Alex, a handsome, blue-eyed, beautiful little boy who was perfect in every way. In the letter that accompanied the pictures, his sweet mother wrote:

> Elder Featherstone:
>
> Thank you for the prayers and counsel you gave me and Cameron when we were pregnant with Alex. No matter what body he had been blessed with, we would be happy to have this choice spirit. Alex loves to smell the flowers, touch, feel, and learn. He loves life and brings happiness to those around him.

On the back of one of the pictures, this couple had written, "Elder Featherstone, I came down to a healthy body and am happy that my parents chose to have me, even though doctors advised of the risks and the 90 percent chance of my having neurological disorders. I love life. —Alexander."

The prayerful, thoughtful decision of that couple meant for Alex life in a sweet, beautiful home with adoring parents. That gift of life is a Christmas gift that will give pleasure every day of his life to both Alex and his parents—and, eventually, to the others who come into this faithful family. Oh, how some of them do *sparkle*.

If putting Christ into Christmas does anything, it teaches us that when we make charity the very essence of our lives, we sparkle. For years I have attempted to really understand charity. I even wrote a book about it—*Charity Never Faileth*—but when I was finished with all of the research and all of the writing, I still did not fully understand the meaning of charity. With each succeeding book I have written, I have included a chapter on charity—feeling that at last I would understand. But after reading and rereading each chapter, I knew I had *still* not wrapped my mind and heart fully around the principle of charity.

I think I do finally understand. Charity is an absolute and total submissiveness to God; it is doing what Christ would do in every circumstance. The very essence of the gospel is charity.

Charity is kind, not cruel. It is a help, not a hindrance. It seeks to repair, not to exact vengeance. It is humble, not harmful.

Charity is forgiving and forgetting. Charity seeks not her own. It is selfless, not self-serving. It seeks to build, not to tear down. Mercy is the essence of charity, and mercy demands nothing in exchange. When people are buried to their neck in trials and heartache, mercy and charity come powerfully together to bring hope.

Over the years, I have been privileged to quietly watch the highest, most noble acts of charity. As Saints in Christ's true Church, we surely ought to be involved in loving, serving, caring, sharing, building up, reducing suffering, and bringing peace and kindness to those around us.

During the Christmas season, our thoughts turn to a star. There are hundreds of billions of stars in the cosmos, but during this season, we think of only one—the star of Bethlehem. It still shines today. The unbeliever does not see it, but it is there. Its radiant beams still shine in our hearts, and we feel the profoundness of its message. Just imagine: Of all the creations of God, one star was set in motion by His Almighty hand and had the sacred privilege of announcing the birth of His Only Begotten Son. No wonder Bethlehem's star shone so brightly—it had a glorious mission to perform.

In wondering awe, we consider the majesty of that one star shining over Bethlehem, announcing the single most important Birth. We may not see that particular star, but we see other stars, shining just as brightly in the eyes of his Saints at Christmastime. Christmas will always be a special and humbly tender time.

Angels still sing "Glory to God in the Highest" and "Joy to the World," but precious few can hear the heavenly strains. Can you comprehend the privilege of being selected to sing in that heavenly choir? Imagine how magnificent that special choir sounded on that night of nights. Imagine, too, the thrill of those who heard the heavenly choirs—singing music composed and prepared especially for an angelic choir to sing on that holy night; music that had the approbation of the Great, Almighty God of heaven and earth; music that thrilled as no other music ever has.

Most will not hear that heavenly choir, but for all of us, Christmas is a time when heavenly music is sung by earthly choirs. It is a time when heaven bows to earth and brightens every good and worthy soul. The spirit of Christmas reaches deep within us and pervades the innermost recesses of our hearts and souls with charity, love, and purity. We reach out with our hearts to the widow, the orphan, the afflicted, the poor, the lonely, and all who struggle with the daily companions of sorrow and despair.

Those of us who believe in Christmas see it sparkle in the eyes of our children. We see it sparkle along the branches of our trees, in the tender strains of carols, in our homes and in our families. Most of all, Christmas sparkles in our hearts as we adore our Savior and King.

As we see and recognize that sparkle, we receive heaven's great gift. And with that gift, oh, how all of us can sparkle.

TOM: THE ORPHAN CHRISTMAS

Tom's father died when he was three
    And thus he lived in poverty.
This little Tom, and Mother, too,
    Were poor and hungry, chilled clear through.
They lived a life of sorrow and tears
    Till the mother died in a few short years.
This orphan, Tom, was now but eight,
    Left to himself, to his lonely fate.
He wandered through the streets alone,
    Ragged and cold, the beggars' clone.
The hunger that Tom bore was great
    No friends he had, nor e'en a mate.

Each day from refuse did Tom eat;
    At night he sheltered on the street.
His hollow eyes and sallow skin
    From a hopeless life, and not from sin.
In poverty, this growing lad
    Was aware of those who never had.
Not food, nor home, nor sheltered place;
    They knew not God, nor His grace,

And met each day with ne'er a hope,
    With no existence but to grope.
So Tom decided that he would
    Be kind and pure and sweet and good.

When Tom was fifteen and winter came,
He walked as an old man, bent and lame.
His tragic life had taken its toll;
    The poor boy's life a beggar's role.
Although his body seemed gaunt and weak,
    His splendid spirit was far less bleak.
He ministered to orphans who, like he,
    Were homeless and cold, in poverty.
From what little he had he always shared;
    Orphan and widow knew Tom cared.
Tom tried to make their burdens light;
    He ministered in love and pure delight.

Christmastime was quickly coming,
    And Tom could hear the merchants humming
Over the business that Christmas brought,
    Tom wondered what the Master thought.
Tom tended to those he'd tried to aid
    Knowing that some were so afraid
That they might not live another year,
    But would die alone, with no one near.
Tom sang them carols loud and clear;
    His melodic voice removed all fear.
He begged and appealed from those who passed
    And shared with all, while it did last.

The Light of Hope

He braced himself against the snow
    And knew not where on earth to go.
'Twas Christmas Eve, having done all he could,
    So he went to church, as Christians should.
In humble rags he knelt and prayed
    That the works of Christ would be displayed
In the lives of orphans and widow friends
    While time does last and love extends.
Tom felt a radiant glow deep in his soul;
    It warmed him through and made him whole.
With Christmas shining in his eyes,
    He left the church to the orphans' cries.

Trusting God in his pure, sweet heart,
    He saw not the horse nor the wagon cart
That struck him down in the cold, dry snow,
    And crushed his chest 'neath the wheels below.
The driver tried to rescue him,
    But the cart was heavy, and the task was grim.
There was no one there to move the load
    Or even help Tom from off the road.
The driver lifted with all his might
    And finally removed Tom's body slight.
He shuddered as he knew the hurt
    Of this youth in worn-out pants and shirt.

He knew that Tom was sure to die,
    So he laid him near the roadside by.
Then from Heaven came a strange, sweet voice
    And a holy light shone round this Pilgrim choice.

Tom opened his eyes, looking far away—
   "Mother!" he said, "Keep talking, please stay.
The eight short years I lived with you
   Was the only love I ever knew.
But I tried to help each orphaned soul,
   And served the widows with my being whole.
Please, Mother, can I now come with you?
   I think I'll die in a minute or two."

"Yes, dear Tom, come home to me,
   And we will joy in Eternity."
Tom closed his eyes as death did creep
   Over the youth about to sleep.
For his life's mission had ended quick—
   He had served the hungry, the cold, and sick.
And just as he breathed his final breath,
   A voice from heaven marked well his death.
"Tom, my son, you are blessed by Me,
   For all thou hast done in charity.
Ye have done it unto the least of mine,
   And behold, my promises are thine.
Thou hast filled life's mission true and well.
   Come, my young friend, and with Me dwell."

Then Tom felt the Savior's sweet embrace
   And saw love and compassion on His face.
Tom smiled, and tears bedimmed his eyes;
   Then lo, to his wondrous and great surprise
His rags were gone, and in their place,
   Royal garments of elegance and grace.

Some like Tom suffer this life through,
    And lose all hope, and reason, too,
But God doth know the burdens they bear
    And hath sent Lord Jesus to love and care.

SUB FOR SANTA

"Then shall the king say unto them on his right hand, come ye blessed of my father, inherit the kingdom prepared for you from the foundation of the world. For I was an hungered and ye gave me meat: I was thirsty and ye gave me drink: I was a stranger and ye took me in: naked and ye clothed me: I was sick and ye visited me: I was in prison and ye came unto me" (Matt. 25:34-35).

As Christmas approached, a pair of humble home teachers were particularly worried about one of the families they visited. This woman and her two children had been abandoned by her husband. Fiercely proud, she was not willing to ask for help, even though it was desperately needed. Even though her home teachers were welcomed in her home, she was not active in the Church and would not accept anything the Church offered. When the home teachers suggested getting her some assistance from the bishop, she refused. It was not a possibility, she firmed responded.

Wanting to help, but not wanting to violate the trust she had in them, the home teachers pondered how they could help. Finally they decided on a plan. They approached many members of the ward, explained the woman's situation, and collected financial contributions from her generous neighbors.

The home teachers then cut a round hole in the end of a large can and in its lid, then cut a slit in one side of the can. They taped all the bills they had collected end-to-end; there were $1, $5, $10, $20, $50, and $100 bills. The home teachers had a delightful time as they alternated the valuable bills; there was more than $1,000, all in different denominations.

These faithful home teachers then rolled the money on a spindle, put the spindle in the can, and sealed the can with the lid. They pulled the first bill through the slit in the side and attached a note that said, "This is a gift from Santa Claus. Use it whenever you need a little cash. Have a Merry Christmas. You are loved."

Several weeks before Christmas, the woman found the gift wrapped in colorful Christmas paper on her front porch. She opened the wrapping paper and found the can. To her astonishment, she saw the money sticking out of the can. She pulled on the $5 bill and found that it was attached to a $20 bill—which was attached to a $1 bill, which was attached to a $50 bill.

It would have been interesting to have seen the expression of gratitude on her face. Now she could buy her children something for Christmas, take care of expenses, and put warm, wholesome food on the table. Her wonderful home teachers lovingly served as a substitute for Santa that year.

I've seen many such tender expressions of care, and through them I have seen experiences that have changed lives. Years ago, I taught early-morning seminary; one mid-November morning, we decided we would sub for Santa for a family. We were able to find a family with eight children, ranging in age from two to the upper teens, that was having severe financial problems. The students were excited at the prospect of helping this family!

I put a bottle on my desk, and we started collecting money. Quite often the students would go without lunch and contribute that money to our fund. The bottle began to fill, and we had quite a large sum of money. On a cold, brisk morning during the second week in December, I went to the locked cupboard in the seminary classroom where we kept our sub for Santa money. I was shocked to find that the bottle was empty. Someone had stolen all the money.

That morning as the students entered, they saw the empty bottle sitting on the desk. I told them what had happened, and asked what we should do. They said, "We will fill it again." That day I suppose all of us—even the teacher—went without lunch. All contributed generously.

We knew the names, ages, and the approximate sizes of the children. We asked students to bring things for the individual children—clothing they had outgrown, coats, toys, and other presents. Two or three days before Christmas, a select committee of students took the money we had raised and went shopping. Those students treated that money as if it were the "widow's mite." They bought a special toy or gift for each of the children and returned to the chapel.

We had been wrapping the gifts we had received, and we were delighted to see that there were new and nearly new coats, clothing, and toys. By the time Christmas Eve arrived, all the gifts were wrapped and tagged with a name; there were gifts for each family member, including the mother and father. We met at 6 p.m. on Christmas Eve, sang a few carols, knelt and had a prayer, and felt a wonderful outpouring of the Christmas spirit. One of the students donned a borrowed Santa outfit, and we started out.

The family lived down a long lane. We took several cars and drove slowly, as quietly as we could, down the lane with our headlights off. We parked a short distance from the house and quietly unloaded the presents onto the front porch. There were boxes filled with them. When all the gifts were piled on the porch, Santa Claus knocked on the door.

One of the younger children opened the door. Staring at Santa with wonder-filled eyes, he cried, "Mom, come quick! It's old Santa Claus! It's him; it's really him!"

Santa Claus gazed around the living room. A humble tree with few decorations stood in the corner; there was nothing under the tree except a few oranges. Santa visited with the family members individually and had a sweet experience. As he concluded his visits, Santa Claus said, "Run to the porch and bring in the presents that are there!" The children stared in amazement at the boxes of presents, then finally began to take them in and nestle them around the tree. As they were absorbed in carrying and arranging the presents, Santa quietly slipped out of the house. Only the parents saw him leave.

We drove back to the chapel. The young man who had worn the Santa suit told the others, "When that little boy said, 'It's old Santa Claus; it's him, it's really him!' I had to hold back the tears." He shared with us what had happened in the house, and we all went home feeling just a little closer to God—and especially closer to the Savior. It was a Christmas none of us will forget.

I remember other similar experiences. A northern Utah man was about 90 percent finished with a house he was building for his family when he passed away; his wife had little money to finish the home and still had the demands of taking care of her family. The elders quorum and high priests group provided some help, but there were still some things left undone.

When her predicament was brought to the attention of the youth in our ward, they voted to make this woman and her children their sub for Santa family. They raised enough money to carpet the house, and a representative group from our ward, along with a member of the bishopric, drove to northern Utah a day or two before Christmas. They presented her with a large check and explained that carpeting for her home was their gift as their sub for Santa project. It's not difficult to imagine how overwhelmed, overcome, and deeply humbled she was. Having recently lost her husband, she had felt tremendous loneliness and despair—only to find that an unknown youth group from Sandy cared enough to raise the money to carpet her home, sharing of themselves to brighten Christmas for her and her children.

The next year the same ward youth group was trying to find a family to sub for Santa. My wife was in the Young Women presidency. She came home after the group's meeting and said, "You get around quite a bit; do you know of a needy family we could sub for Santa?"

I thought for a minute and told her I knew the perfect family—a couple that lived in our ward boundaries with their two teenaged daughters. None of them was a member of the Church.

"But they do well financially," Merlene objected. "They have a lovely home, and they're not in need. The daughters are wonderful, and the parents take good care of them."

"When you sub for Santa, you give gifts," I explained. "Can you think of a more wonderful gift to give to Dick, Kathy, and their two girls than the gospel? What if the youth committee had a special prayer and fast that this family would be baptized on Christmas Eve? The youth could fast each Sunday until Christmas, and I think God would help answer their prayers. I think His Spirit would touch the family for whom the youth are praying. Such a gift would be the gift of self—not a worldly or material gift."

She thought the idea was good, and during the next meeting she raised the idea about giving the gift of baptism—of membership in the Lord's only true and living Church—on Christmas Eve. She didn't say anything else; she wanted the youth to choose the family and make the plans.

The youth were excited about the idea and started discussing which family they wanted to serve. Finally someone suggested, "Why not the Bowmans? Their two daughters come to Mutual." Immediately everyone knew they had chosen the right family.

They made all the plans, making sure they involved the bishop and the full-time missionaries. A committee of youth went to see the bishop; after rehearsing what they had done the previous year, they asked for his approval of the Bowmans as their new sub for Santa family.

"They live fairly close to me," the bishop said, after listening patiently to them. "They don't need anything financially, and they are not members of the Church."

"We know they are not members of the Church, but that would be our sub for Santa gift to them," one of the boys responded. "We would baptize them on Christmas Eve into the Lord's Church."

"All the youth are going to fast and pray to bring them into the Church," another youth explained, "and we're going to invite the entire ward to join in our fasting and prayer."

The bishop thought about it for a minute, then replied, "You know, I think that's wonderful. It's a great idea. I agree."

"Great!" the youth committee leader said. "Now we need your help, Bishop. Would you have the Bowman family come to your office, and will you tell them that all the youth are fasting and praying that they will be baptized on Christmas Eve?"

I wasn't there, but I can imagine the bishop, wondering how he ever got involved in this and perhaps even feeling a little trapped. After long deliberation, he finally agreed to invite Dick, Kathy, and their two daughters to his office.

From what I heard, the Bowmans arrived—Dick was in a suit, and Kathy and the girls in their Sunday best. The bishop welcomed them, told them about the previous year's youth sub for Santa and then announced, "This year they have selected your family to sub for Santa."

Dick and Kathy exchanged confused glances; certainly they didn't need help providing Christmas for their daughters. The bishop then explained that the youth had determined that as their gift, they would fast and pray all through December that the Bowmans would be baptized on Christmas Eve.

"The most precious thing the youth felt they could give you as a gift was baptism into the Lord's Church," the bishop concluded. "What do you think about that?"

Imagine how this wonderful man and his wife felt when they learned what the youth in the ward were willing to do for them. Dick looked at Kathy, then at his children; it was clear that the entire family was touched. Finally Dick responded, "I think that would be fine."

The youth arranged for the missionaries to teach the family, and they carried out their plan of fasting and praying.

On Christmas Eve, Dick, Kathy, and their two daughters stood at the baptismal font, dressed in white. The eve before we celebrated the birth of Christ, these four wonderful pilgrims were baptized. The ward had never had a whiter Christmas . . . until a year later, when this wonderful family of four gathered in the temple. That day they were all dressed in celestial white, and one having the authority sealed them for time and for all eternity.

As we have been told in holy writ, whatsoever is sealed on earth shall be sealed in heaven. Through their faith and their willingness to give of themselves, those youth shared the greatest gift imaginable, both in mortality and throughout the eternities. It was the most precious sub for Santa any of us have ever participated in.

AT CHRISTMAS TIME

How white the night at Christmastime,
    With carols sung in strains sublime;
And falls the snow so pure and white
    On Christmas night, on Christmas night.

For, lo, the star bent low to earth
    Announcing Jesus' royal birth;
The stem of Jesse, Israel's rod,
    Emmanuel, the Son of God.

Shepherds, wise men all were there,
    The stable bleak was cold and bare;
A halo round the infant shone,
    And Mary loved her very own.

It's Christmas morn; it's Christmas morn!
    The holy Son of God is born,
When all the world wakes up and sings,
    The Son of God, the King of Kings!

It's Christmas here; it's Christmas there;
  It's joyous Christmas everywhere!
Let bells ring out in wild acclaim
  His holy blessed birth proclaim.

CHRISTMAS EVERYWHERE

Phillip Brooks wrote a beautiful poem titled "Christmas Everywhere," and its message applies to all of us as we approach the Christmas season:

Everywhere, everywhere, Christmas tonight!
Christmas in lands of the fir tree and pine,
Christmas in lands of the palm tree and vine,
Christmas where snow peaks stand solemn and white,
Christmas where cornfields stand sunny and bright.
Christmas where children are hopeful and gay,
Christmas where old men are patient and gray,
Christmas where peace, like a dove in flight,
Broods over brave men in the thick of the fight
Everywhere, everywhere, Christmas tonight.

For the Christ child who comes is the Master of all;
No palace too great, no cottage too small.
    (Phillip Brooks, *Christmas Songs and Easter Carols* [New York: E.P. Dutton & Co., 1903]).

Yes, Christmas is everywhere—no palace too great, no cottage too small. A few years ago I asked if I could speak at each of the different facilities at the Utah State Prison during December. I considered it a great privilege to talk about Christ, the babe in Bethlehem, and all that Christmas represents. The most humbling part of that experience was visiting the women's prison.

Several dozen women came to the meeting. I shared with them my own Christmas experiences. I told about the Christmas when I wanted a coat—the Christmas when I learned to appreciate the sacrifices my mother made for our family. I told about the Christmas when we couldn't afford a tree until Christmas Eve, when the tree lots slashed their prices dramatically; we got a six-foot tree for seventy-five cents. I rehearsed the way my Uncle Ernest came to our home Christmas Eve, and described how we children would press up against the window waiting for him to come.

In addition to sharing my humble personal stories, I talked about the real meaning of Christmas—and told the women that traditional gifts in wrapping paper and ribbons are not essential for a wonderful Christmas. I read from Matthew 25, and was moved to tears several times during that recitation.

Then a wonderful thing happened. It was as though I were talking to a Relief Society at a meetinghouse; a sweet, humble, Christmas spirit filled that little meeting room at the penitentiary. The sisters wept, and I could feel a special tenderness there. It was a precious moment, and I knew then that Christmas—along with its distinctive spirit—is everywhere.

I once read a sweet story of contrasts related to the thought that Christmas is everywhere:

It was Christmas eve. In our neighbor's beautiful home every room was ablaze with light. Merry guests flitted about, and in the kitchen servants with white aprons and trim caps bustled around getting ready for the evening's merrymaking. In the center of the drawing room was the tree; it stood loaded down with costly presents and colored candles. On the sideboards in the dining rooms, and on the tables in the kitchen were boxes of candy, nuts, and fruits.

Master Cecil Barclay, the seven-year-old son of the house, wandered up and down stairs, from room to room, with his hands and pockets full of things, all too good, perhaps, for one little boy. He was impatient for the tree to be lighted.

At last, when the guests were assembled, the dear old saint of this blessed time came in. His coat was flecked with snow flakes, and his merry eyes twinkled as he made his bow and began his work on the tree.

It seemed that he would never cease from calling Cecil's name. Books and balls, toys, useful and otherwise, sleds, and skates, things to wear and things to eat, came to the lot of the little boy. He took each new parcel with a look of interest, but soon laid it aside.

When the candles had burned out and the people were in the great dining room, Cecil was sitting in the corner surrounded by his Christmas presents. His hands held a half-eaten orange while nearby was a bag of rich candy.

His mother found him there, crying. "What is the matter, my child?" said she. The boy glanced about, and putting both sticky hands to his eyes sobbed out: "I want something else."

* * * * *

In our little home on the opposite corner of this same block, my two little brothers had gone hopefully to bed. My mother was sitting by the table, her head bowed. It was a very sad Christmas time for us. We were poorer than ever before, and Mother had told the boys that perhaps our good wishes and love for each other would be all our Christmas offerings this year. She could not bear to see the children disappointed, but we had tried in vain to eke out enough even for the simplest present.

We thought the boys were asleep when the outer door opened, and something was thrust inside. Before we could reach the door, Ted was out of his bed, and had the little red wagon in his hands. There was a book for Don and a pair of skates for each of them. A basket filled with dainty food bore the card of the dressmaker for whom I worked.

Mother's face lighted up so! The boys fairly screamed in their delight, and then stopped short to kneel by the bed and thank God for Santa Claus.

One block apart! One little child of that Christ who came to beautify the world at this His birthtime surrounded by so much and still crying out for "something else"; and two other little ones of this selfsame Savior falling on their knees and blessing Him for so little.

Oh, wonderful Christmas spirit that helps so many of us to see what we have, which He in His love has given, and thank Him for it all, nor cry out in our surfeited childish impatience for "something else" ("One Block Apart," *Young Women's Journal,* Vol. 12, Dec. 1901).

That kind of gratitude doesn't just happen on the pages of books written a century ago. I've witnessed it myself and know that Christmas *is* everywhere, even in the farthest corner of the world. One year my wife and son Paul accompanied me to the Philippines. There we saw a hundred or more children line up to get an apple, an orange, a coloring book, and a few crayons. Most of the children had never seen a large Washington Red Delicious apple. They were so patient to stand and wait, hoping the supply would not run out before their turn came! That Christmas Eve as we returned to our hotel, we felt that we had walked where Jesus walked.

A few miles from where we had helped distribute the gifts to the children is an active eighty-acre garbage dump; an estimated 60,000 people live atop the dump, retrieving wire, metal, telephone books, string, wood, and anything else they can to eke out a living. On Christmas Sunday members of the Tondo Ward come down off the dump, dressed in their Sunday best, to worship Jesus. They sing carols and read about the Savior and pray, thanking God for their blessings. At the conclusion of Church services, they return to their makeshift nipa huts on the dump.

Christmas *is* everywhere. I have often suspected that Santa Claus misses the little children who live on that garbage dump, but I know with all my heart that Jesus does not miss them.

Yes, it's Christmas everywhere, but Christmas sometimes has a different meaning in places where children may receive so little. Gratitude sometimes appears to be in inverse relationship to the number of gifts received—those who receive very little may often consider the smallest gift an absolute treasure. But it doesn't have to be that way: Those who receive much can also feel deep gratitude.

Poverty or riches are not what make us grateful; gratitude stems from a conviction and witness that all gifts come from God. Mother Teresa is a wonderful example: In her poverty, when she had nothing, she shared with others and gave herself to the needy. Hers was an expression of the Christmas spirit wherever she went, every day of the year.

Yes, Christmas is everywhere—but it takes each one of us to put the spirit into Christmas, to give freely of ourselves and to receive with gratitude, to put our love of the Savior into each thing we do and each gift we give. As we prepare for this Christmas season, may we always remember, in the tender sentiments of Phillip Brooks, "Everywhere, everywhere, Christmas tonight!"

THE INFANT KING

Sing Noel at Christmas time,
    Let all the bells in heaven chime.
Praise the stem of Jesse's rod—
    The newborn King, the Son of God.
The Child thus born as God's own Son
    Will ransom all; yes, every one.
The angels sang while shepherds saw
    As mild He lay in tufted straw.
The Babe from royal lineage springs.
    Christ has come; all heaven sings.
The wise men come the great long way,
    Their homage and their gifts to pay.
For lo, this lowly Son of birth
Will rule as King o'er heaven and earth.

CHRISTMAS—ILLUSION OR REALITY

It is estimated that the Milky Way galaxy contains 600 billion stars. We have identified more than twenty such galaxies, and some astronomers suggest there are at least 600 billion galaxies we have not yet identified.

If the God of heaven can place billions of stars throughout the immensity of space, is it unreasonable to think that He could place a brilliant new star in the skies directly over Bethlehem to announce the birth of His Only Begotten Son? Could it be that such a star was placed in that midnight sky so that all men who lifted up their eyes could realize that He who was born could lift all men?

Would it be beyond our comprehension to believe that on the American continent, Christ's birth was marked by a day and a night and a day without any darkness? Perhaps that day and night and day of light can remind us that His birth ushered in the dawning of eternal blessings for all mankind.

Would anyone suppose that at the mortal death of the Savior, God could not cause three nights and days of the most intense darkness—a darkness so dense that no light could penetrate it? Maybe those three days and nights of total darkness remind us that without repentance there is no light—no way to penetrate the darkness.

In mortality we move from one year to the next in what seems to be a perpetual cycle. Yet some seem to ascend to increasingly higher levels, moving ever heavenward as they progress from year to year; they are the ones who accept the divine will of God and endeavor to keep His commandments. Others move from year to year in the same cycle, but their choices take them in the opposite direction, sinking them increasingly deeper into sadness, sin, and misery.

As we move from one year to the next, we should ever strive to look heavenward. As the year draws to a close and another Christmas approaches, it is for me the most spiritual Christmas of my life. There seems to be a mellowing and softening influence. I have become aware of many kind deeds that have moved me deeply. I seem to feel closer to the Savior than ever before, and I have realized that gifts given are more fulfilling and rewarding than gifts received. I have come to understand as never before that time spent with those we love is far more precious than the money we spend on expensive gifts.

This year I have discovered that things I have previously accepted as real were instead nothing more than illusion. As an example, consider the illusions and realities that abound in the example of Aaron and the Lamanite king:

> And it came to pass that after Aaron had expounded these things unto him, the king said: What shall I do that I may have this eternal life of which thou hast spoken? Yea, what shall I do that I may be born of God, having this wicked spirit rooted out of my breast, and receive his Spirit, that I may be filled with joy, that I may not be cast off at the last day? Behold, said he, I will give up all that I possess, yea, I will forsake my kingdom, that I may receive this great joy.

> But Aaron said unto him: If thou desirest this thing, if thou wilt bow down before God, yea, if thou wilt repent of all thy sins, and will bow down before God, and call on his name in faith, believing that ye shall receive, then shalt thou receive the hope which thou desirest.
>
> And it came to pass that when Aaron had said these words, the king did bow down before the Lord, upon his knees; yea, even he did prostrate himself upon the earth, and cried mightily, saying:
>
> O God, Aaron hath told me that there is a God; and if there is a God, and if thou art God, wilt thou make thyself known unto me, and I will give away all my sins to know thee (Alma 22:15-18).

With his newly gained perspective of eternal things, the king recognized that his authority, his worldly possessions, the "pleasure" he had gained in sin—indeed, his kingship itself—were all an illusion compared to those things that were truly important.

Enos said:

> Behold, it came to pass that I, Enos, knowing my father that he was a just man—for he taught me in his language, and also in the nurture and admonition of the Lord—and blessed be the name of my God for it—

And I will tell you of the wrestle which I had before God, before I received a remission of my sins.

Behold, I went to hunt beasts in the forests; and the words which I had often heard my father speak concerning eternal life, and the joy of the saints, sunk deep into my heart.

And my soul hungered; and I kneeled down before my Maker, and I cried unto him in mighty prayer and supplication for mine own soul; and all the day long did I cry unto him; yea, and when the night came I did still raise my voice high that it reached the heavens.

And there came a voice unto me, saying: Enos, thy sins are forgiven thee, and thou shalt be blessed.

And I, Enos, knew that God could not lie; wherefore, my guilt was swept away.

And I said: Lord, how is it done?

And he said unto me: Because of thy faith in Christ, whom thou hast never before heard nor seen. And many years pass away before he shall manifest himself in the flesh; wherefore, go to, thy faith hath made thee whole (Enos 1:1-8).

The great tempter cries out, "Eat, drink, and be merry, for tomorrow you die." But we know that he lies, and we know that indulgence never was happiness. Money may allow us to accumulate valuable assets, but it can never buy peace. Peace is not an illusion; it is the result of a humble submission to the Master's will. It is the result of unwavering faith in Christ. As with the king of the Lamanites, so with Enos. Do you suppose either would have traded his experience for all the acclaim or money that could be bestowed upon them?

Alma rehearsed with his righteous son Helaman the contrast between illusion and reality when he told of his wayward days as a youth and "the change" that was wrought in his life:

> For I went about with the sons of Mosiah, seeking to destroy the church of God; but behold, God sent his holy angel to stop us by the way.
>
> And behold, he spake unto us, as it were the voice of thunder, and the whole earth did tremble beneath our feet; and we all fell to the earth, for the fear of the Lord came upon us.
>
> But behold, the voice said unto me: Arise. And I arose and stood up, and beheld the angel.
>
> And he said unto me: If thou wilt of thyself be destroyed, seek no more to destroy the church of God.

And it came to pass that I fell to the earth; and it was for the space of three days and three nights that I could not open my mouth, neither had I the use of my limbs.

And the angel spake more things unto me, which were heard by my brethren, but I did not hear them; for when I heard the words—If thou wilt be destroyed of thyself, seek no more to destroy the church of God—I was struck with such great fear and amazement lest perhaps I should be destroyed, that I fell to the earth and I did hear no more.

But I was racked with eternal torment, for my soul was harrowed up to the greatest degree and racked with all my sins.

Yea, I did remember all my sins and iniquities, for which I was tormented with the pains of hell; yea, I saw that I had rebelled against my God, and that I had not kept his holy commandments.

Yea, and I had murdered many of his children, or rather led them away unto destruction; yea, and in fine so great had been my iniquities, that the very thought of coming into the presence of my God did rack my soul with inexpressible horror.

Oh, thought I, that I could be banished and become extinct both soul and body, that I might not be brought to stand in the presence of my God, to be judged of my deeds.

And now, for three days and for three nights was I racked, even with the pains of a damned soul.

And it came to pass that as I was thus racked with torment, while I was harrowed up by the memory of my many sins, behold, I remembered also to have heard my father prophesy unto the people concerning the coming of one Jesus Christ, a Son of God, to atone for the sins of the world.

Now, as my mind caught hold upon this thought, I cried within my heart: O Jesus, thou Son of God, have mercy on me, who am in the gall of bitterness, and am encircled about by the everlasting chains of death.

And now, behold, when I thought this, I could remember my pains no more; yea, I was harrowed up by the memory of my sins no more.

And oh, what joy, and what marvelous light I did behold; yea, my soul was filled with joy as exceeding as was my pain!

Yea, I say unto you, my son, that there could be nothing so exquisite and so bitter as were my pains. Yea, and again I say unto you, my son, that on the other hand, there can be nothing so exquisite and sweet as was my joy.

Yea, methought I saw, even as our father Lehi saw, God sitting upon his throne, surrounded with numberless concourses of angels, in the attitude of singing and praising their God; yea, and my soul did long to be there (Alma 36:6-22).

At this Christmas season we ought to remember that no gift we have ever received or could ever receive will surpass the wondrous gift of the Atonement. Our joy can be exquisite and sweet, and we have a promise of being in the presence of God. What greater gift in all the world could we hope for? In return, we ought to determine to give all we can to the Savior of all mankind—our total heart and soul, even our very being.

Leon Hartshorn included the story of the Swinyards and "The Christmas We Gave Away" in his memorable Christmas book.

> The Christmas I remember best began with tragedy. It happened at 6 a.m. on one of those crisp Idaho Falls mornings the day before Christmas. Our neighbors, the Jesse Smith family, slept peacefully in their two-story home. The baby, barely six months old, was in a crib next to her parents' room, and the three older children were upstairs.
>
> Suddenly something jarred Jesse from his sleep. He thought he smelled smoke. Could a spark from the torch he'd defrosted the frozen water

pipes with the day before have started a fire in the basement? Still half asleep, he stumbled to the bedroom door and flung it open. Clouds of black smoke poured into the room. "Lorraine!" he yelled. "Get the baby!" He ran toward the stairs and his sleeping children. The smoke was thicker as he gasped for breath. "Rick! Tom! Wake up!" The boys scrambled out of their beds. "Run, boys!" Tom grabbed his younger brother's hand, and they raced down the smoke-filled stairway to safety. His daughter's room was next. As Jesse groped through the heavy shroud of gray, he called, "Cindy! Cindy! Where are you?"

"Here, Daddy, here!" He followed the frightened cries, scooped up his daughter in his arms, and with his hand over her face, felt his way out of the room and down through a narrow path of searing flames. They coughed, choked, gasped for breath, until they at last stumbled out the door where a relieved wife and three children stood shivering in the snow.

Now the family looked to the smoke and flames pouring out the roof of their home, the home that the night before had held all their earthly treasures. It had also held a promise of Christmas, mulled cider, homemade candy, and stockings waiting to be filled. They stood huddled in their nightclothes, barefoot in the biting cold, and watched their Christmas burn up along with their house.

The spell was broken by the sound of sirens. . . . Firemen leaped from the huge red trucks and turned their powerful hoses on the blaze. Seconds later, the bishop of the Smiths' ward drove up, bundled the family into his car, and took them to a home the ward elders quorum had just completed as a fund-raising project. They were not to witness the firemen's hopeless battle with the flames. For when the trucks finally pulled away, this time in silence, nothing stood of their house but its charred skeleton outlined against the sky.

And tomorrow was Christmas. At our house we were putting the last secret wrappings on the presents, making the last batch of popcorn for popcorn balls to go in our Christmas stockings. We three children were attempting dubious harmony with our favorite carols and breaking into giggles at the results.

Then Dad came in with the news. We sat with serious faces listening to him tell of the fire, the narrow escape, the house where the Smiths were spending Christmas Eve.

"Why?" Mother said. "Why did this happen, just at Christmas? It isn't fair. They have children, just

The Light of Hope

the same ages as ours," she said. Jesse and Dad were the closest friends; they even joked that they were so close they wore the same size shirt. The same size shirt! "Bill," Mother began hesitantly, "would you mind terribly if we gave Jesse one of the shirts I bought you for Christmas? You wear the same size. . . ."

A hush fell on us all. We all seemed to be thinking the exact same thing. "I've got it!" my ten-year-old brother shouted. "We'll give the Smiths a Christmas! A Christmas for Christmas!" "Where could we get one?" my inquisitive little sister asked. "We'll give them ours," the others chorused in.

"Of course! We'll give them ours!" The house rang with excited voices, until Dad's stern command silenced us. "Hold it! Let's make sure we all want to do this. Let's take a vote. All in favor say aye."

"*AYE!*" chorused back at him. "All opposed?" was met with silence. The hours that followed are ones we will never forget. First we sat around the tree and handed out presents. Instead of opening them, the giver would divulge their contents so the label could be changed to the appropriate Smith family member. My heart fell when Dad handed Kevin a box wrapped in gold foil and green ribbon. "It's a baseball glove, son," Dad told him, and a flash of disappointment crossed

Kevin's face. I knew how he'd longed for that glove, and Dad wanted to say, "You keep it, son," but Kevin smiled as if he'd read our thoughts. "Thanks, Dad. It's just what Stan wanted, too." he replied.

"Look, here's the recipe holder I made for you, that is, for Sister Smith." We signed all the tags "From Santa," and the activity that followed would have put his workshop elves to shame.

They had presents, but what about a Christmas dinner? The turkey was cooked, pies baked, the carrots and celery prepared, and then all packed in a box. The Christmas stockings must be stuffed. Dad got a length of clothesline and some clothespins to hang the stockings with, but what about a tree? We looked at ours. Could we really part with it? "I know," Dad volunteered. "Let's decorate it with things they'll need." And so many things were added to the tree: a tube of toothpaste tied with red ribbon, a razor, comb, bars of soap nestled in the branches. Finally it was all ready.

It was a strange procession that silently paraded through the dark streets of Idaho Falls that night. Father led the way carrying a fully decorated tree. Mother followed with a complete Christmas dinner, down to the last dish of cranberry sauce. The three of us children pulled wagons and a sled piled with boxes of gifts. We waited until the last light was out in the Smiths' borrowed home, and then Mom and Dad stealthily carried each item in the door. When the last stocking had been hung, we turned again toward home.

All the way home I worried about what waited for my family at our home. What if the others were disappointed? All that was left were a few pine needles and paper scraps. I couldn't have been more wrong. The minute we were back inside we were more excited than ever. Every pine needle and paper scrap was a reminder of the magic of the evening, and we hadn't taken that to the Smiths. It was in our home as real as if you could see it. A happier family never went to bed on a Christmas Eve, and the next morning the magic was still there. For our celebration we wrote a promise to each person on a card and presented it around a spruce branch tied in a red ribbon.

"One shoe shine. To Father. Love Kevin." "This is good for two turns doing the evening dishes. Love, your husband Bill." And so it went. Our Christmas dinner consisted of scrambled eggs and bacon, toast and sliced oranges. Somehow, I don't remember a better one. And I know we sang our carols that night with the same unconventional harmony, but it sounded sweeter than angels to me.

> "Oh, Mommy," said my small sister as she snuggled up for her bedtime Christmas story, "I like to give Christmases away." Tears blurred the book in my mother's hands, because she knew that none of us would ever forget this Christmas, the one when we gave our best gift. And as she read the story of the Baby born in a manger, it seemed our gift was but a small tribute to him who gave his best gift, his Son to us.

Could there be any question in the minds of any of those children what *Christmas Spirit* really meant? They knew that love, service, caring, compassion, and charity made up the Christmas Spirit—and they knew it in a way none would ever forget. They learned that a table heaped with sumptuous food, a tree boasting decorations and tinsel, a jolly Santa Claus, and a pile of brightly wrapped gifts are all illusions—*unless* they are accompanied by the things that create the Christmas Spirit.

As an assistant to the Twelve Apostles, Elder Gordon B. Hinckley related the story of Hannah Daphne Smith Dalton, who as a little girl lived in Parowan, Utah, with her mother while her father served a mission in Denmark. Remembering her experiences later in her life, Hannah wrote:

> My little mother had to work like a slave to keep her children while Father was on his mission. I remember how every night she would spin, and how in the daytime, I would split fine splinters off from the pitchy wood, and at night I would sit

with her and tend the baby and keep holding and lighting these pitchy sticks for her to see to spin by, and how I would cry when I went to bed to think my sweet little mother had to work so hard. . . .

I remember the Christmas of 1862. All of us children hung up our stockings. We jumped up early in the morning to see what Santa had brought, but there was not a thing in them. Mother wept bitterly. She went to her box and got a little apple and cut it in little tiny pieces and that was our Christmas, but I have never forgotten to this day how I loved her dear little hands as she was cutting that apple (*Conference Report*, April 1959).

Can that kind of love be an illusion? Absolutely not. Can the love of the Savior be an illusion? Unequivocally not. To those who believe, Christmas is real because *Christ* is real.

Consider what is real as I share a letter I received more than two decades ago from a family in Tennessee:

You came to our stake in September and at that time gave a blessing to our daughter Amanda, who has leukemia. This blessing was very specific and greater than my expectations of her being able to endure her infirmities.

Amanda was hospitalized in October because of the toxic effects of chemotherapy. She had severe seizures and lost her sight. However, during this time our thoughts always returned to the blessing you gave.

I must tell you that Satan has tried us as a family during this time. My husband has been unemployed for five months, and we are facing foreclosure on our home. But during this time we have managed to draw close to one another and our faith has been unwavering. . . .

We returned November 1 to Memphis for a check-up and more WIT chemotherapy. This entailed several bone marrow and spinal taps; but routine blood work was done first. They were astounded by what they found. They did one bone marrow test and one spinal tap and found no trace of immature white cells—leukemia!

They opted to stop chemotherapy and sent us home. We arrived home very late with our wonderful news. Amanda insisted on going to school even though she had slept only a few hours. She wanted to tell her friends she didn't take "drugs" anymore.

Well, after school that day Amanda's teacher called, asking if I could explain something Amanda said during sharing time. She told her class this: "I won't lose my hair anymore, and I don't have no more leukemia because this man who is a friend of the prophet gave me a blessing that made me better." Needless to say, she wanted to know who this man was, and what prophet Amanda was talking about! This opened the door for me as a missionary.

Brother Featherstone, I want to thank you with all my heart for being worthy to give such blessings. The six years I've had Amanda have been beautiful ones, but now, because of you and the priesthood, I will be able to treasure many more. Thank you.

As members of His true Church, we have been given the priesthood of God—the authority to act in His name. It is God who heals the sick. The healing powers are not ours, but we can be in the right place and can live the kind of pure, sweet life that enables us to act in His name. As I read that letter that day, I wept a few tears before offering a silent prayer. I knew that the doctors could not heal Amanda. I knew that Vaughn Featherstone certainly could not heal Amanda. (Every priesthood holder knows he is clinging to an illusion if he supposes he himself is the healer.) But I knew that the priesthood of God is His power—and I knew that exercising the priesthood of God in worthiness and faith can cause healing to take place if that is His will. That is not an illusion. It is a simple, eternal reality.

A dozen years later my secretary announced that a young woman wanted to see me. Amanda Cunningham, then eighteen years old and a member of both the state championship tennis team and the state championship cross country team, walked in and hugged me.

"Thank you, Elder Featherstone, for living in such a way the Lord could bless me through you," she smiled. Here stood a beautiful, healthy young woman who understood that Jesus Christ is not an illusion, but a reality—that He is a God of miracles, and that the Christmas Spirit as it comes from Christ actually happens all year long.

What a beautiful description of reality. Those who have faith become sanctified and purified through their trials.

A beautiful illustration of that reality occurred in the life of Elder Robert L. Simpson. On the first Thursday of December, all the General Authorities were in the temple for our monthly meeting; President Spencer W. Kimball was the prophet, and he liked to reserve time during each meeting for the bearing of testimonies. Because he only called on two brethren at a time, there wasn't much time to collect your thoughts. I was sitting next to Elder Simpson, and that day, President Kimball announced, "We will next hear from Elder Simpson." I nudged him in the ribs with my elbow. "And he will be followed by Elder Featherstone," President Kimball announced—and I got a quick nudge in my own ribs from Elder Simpson.

Even though I was to follow Elder Simpson and might have been preoccupied with thinking about what I was going to say, his testimony captured and held my interest. I heard every word.

Elder Simpson related that he had been on a mission in New Zealand when Word War II began; he returned home from his mission to face the draft and was quickly drafted into the army. Between his call to military duty and the time he reported, he married, and his wife became pregnant. He knew he would not be able to be present when the baby was born.

Elder Simpson was sent to Egypt and was assigned to work with several companies of soldiers from New Zealand because he spoke Maori. His first Christmas Eve in the military he was alone in the barracks; all the other soldiers had gone out to celebrate, get drunk, and find companionship.

It was the loneliest he had ever felt in his life: He was all alone on Christmas Eve, thousands of miles from home, separated from his wife and a newborn son he had never seen, and uncertain if he would survive the combat to return home alive. He picked up his copy of a Church magazine—which he had already read a dozen times—then put it down with a sigh. Suddenly, off in the distance he heard Christmas music coming from the direction of the Canteen. He decided being with a group of soldiers was better than being alone on Christmas Eve, so he dressed in his officer's uniform and walked across the parade grounds to the Canteen.

As he opened the door, a thick cloud of tobacco smoke belched out toward him. The drunken soldiers inside were loud, vulgar, and not singing the Christmas hymns that he felt were appropriate. He was edging around the perimeter of the room when a man in a Santa suit threw him a package and shouted, "Here, soldier, have a little Christmas cheer!"

Elder Simpson caught the package as he continued to work his way toward the door. Knowing the celebration in the Canteen went against everything he held precious and dear, he made his way back to the barracks and sat on his bunk, feeling lonelier than ever. He looked at the package in his lap for a few minutes before picking at the wrapping paper. It was a fruitcake, four inches wide, four inches high, and a foot long. Attached to the top of the fruitcake was this note:

Dear Soldier,

Wherever you are, have a Merry Christmas. Thank you for fighting for our country, our freedom, and our liberty. We love you. God bless you.

The Relief Society Sisters of the Takami Branch in New Zealand

What are the chances that such a package would get into the hands of a wonderful, clean, pure soldier who had served his mission in New Zealand—and who was now serving in the military, stationed thousands of miles away? Clearly, Jesus Christ, the Savior of all mankind whose birth we celebrate at Christmas, guided that package to Elder Simpson.

Later, I visited the Takami Stake in New Zealand. I told the story of Elder Simpson and the fruitcake, and then asked how many of the sweet sisters in attendance had been in the Takami Branch when the fruitcakes were baked and sent to the soldiers who were then serving in World War II. Four or five gray-haired sisters tearfully raised their hands. "Thank God for you wonderful sisters who blessed Elder Simpson's life," I told them.

Christmas is a reality. The Christmas Spirit of giving and receiving gifts is a reality. Without Christ, toys and tinsel, carols and lights, trees and feasts are all illusion—but *with* Him, they become reality. All of those things of Christmas, and all of those things throughout the year, take on value only when we understand that Jesus Christ was the literal Son of God, and that His birth brought to earth the only soul who would qualify as sinless and perfect and as the Son of God.

MAYBE A CHRISTMAS TREE

The sainted mother watched her flock
    As they prepared for bed.
She only had a little milk
    And one small loaf of bread.
She thought her heart would surely break
    As the children knelt in prayer;
"Dear God, please send a Christmas tree
    So it could stand right there.
We really don't expect a gift
    Or even any food.
We haven't been so very bad,
    But we haven't been so good.
So we dare not ask for very much,
    It wouldn't be quite right.
But maybe just a Christmas tree
    That we could have tonight."
Her daughter's prayer soon ended,
    And she got up off her knees;
The other children hugged her,
    And her mom gave her a squeeze.

She knew the children all had faith,
    But doubted in her own.
For not a single cent had she,
    And she felt all alone.
The children danced and sang
    As they went to climb in bed,
While the mother wrung her hands
    And bowed her weary head.
Tomorrow would be Christmas Eve,
    And she felt such despair.
As she thought about the child
    Who had said the family prayer,
And knew that God would send a tree
    And stand it over there.
Soft tears brushed o'er the mother's cheeks,
    And she sat down in her chair.
And then she heard soft footsteps,
    And knew someone had come.
She hoped it might be old Saint Nick,
    But she feared he wouldn't come.

The snow was falling softly down
    And piling up so deep,
She wondered who had ventured out
    When others were asleep.
She opened the door and standing there
    In snow twelve inches high,
The snow swirled round his friendly face;
    Her heart did joy and sigh.

Her father had come a thousand miles
    To make it there in time;
She cried and hugged and kissed him;
    Her joy was now sublime.
"Of all the men on earth I'd see,
    I'd so desire it to be you!
We haven't much to share right now,
    But I'll always love you true."
He smiled so warmly on her now
    It took away all care.
And then she wept and said, "Father, dear,
    You're an answer to a prayer.
The children prayed for a Christmas tree
    To stand right over there."

His deep brown eyes had moistened,
    And he wiped away a tear.
"My daughter, I've been driving hard,
    Don't you ever fear.
I've been driving for the past three days
    With an unknown urgency;
And now I fathom God's great will;
    I'll get your Christmas tree."
He headed out into the snow,
    The gale was blowing hard;
And several hours later,
    He drove into the yard.
"I've bought a splendid tree," he said,
    "I've got ornaments and lights.

I've got boxes filled with lots of food
    For long, cold winter nights.
I bought each child a special gift,
    And something nice for you."
He laid the treasured gifts all out
    Except for one or two.

He took the tree and placed it where
    The mother told him so.
"I think its ornaments will shine
    When the strings of lights all glow."
She laughed and smiled and humbly said,
    "Dear Dad, I love you so."
With his great hands he held her,
    And said, "Sweetheart, I know."
Then back he went to his old car
    And brought in one last thing.
He laid it down and whispered,
    "It's the treasure of a king."
She tenderly unwrapped her gift
    And to her great surprise,
Was the great old family Bible
    Which brought teardrops to her eyes.
The father held her closer,
    And whispered in her ear:
"When life seemed dark and hopeless,
    We found our strength in here."

He turned a page or two, then stopped,
    And read a scripture best,

"Come unto me all ye that labor,
    And I will give you rest."
Then he said, "The Father of all
    Knew that you were sad;
While sitting in my easy chair,
    There came a voice that said,
'Your daughter prays, has lost all hope,
    Go to her now and give
The strength that she will surely need
    If she is yet to live.
Her children all have prayed this day
    And asked for one small tree,
By sharing with the least of these,
    You'll do it unto me.'"
So the mother sings sweet carols
    And beautifully she sings,
Throughout eternity she'll love
    Our God, the King of Kings.

The Master loved and nurtured her,
    And blessed this mother fair.
She'll always remember one Christmas
    And a heartfelt child's prayer.

PURITY IN CHRISTMAS

I have a wonderful friend who is also a friend to everyone he knows. He is tall and strong and robust; his hair is white as snow. He has worked the soil for his living. His hands are large and calloused and gentle, attesting to a life of working the soil. He has served as a bishop, a stake president, and a Regional Representative. He could serve anywhere at any level in the Church, but he has an unusual spirit of humility and purity that is Christlike. His name is David Harvey, and he lives in Pleasant Grove, Utah.

John Ruskin made a statement that aptly describes David Harvey:

> I believe the test of a great man is humility. I do not mean by humility the doubt in one's own power; but really truly great men have a curious feeling that greatness is not in them but through them and see the divine in every other human soul and are foolishly, endlessly, incredibly merciful.

I am confident that David Harvey does not know what a great soul he is—or how truly special he is.

A few years ago I learned that he was in the hospital recovering from open-heart surgery. I approached his hospital room quietly and saw that he was all alone. I stood and watched this marvelous, white-haired Saint as he lay in bed asleep. He looked angelic—pure and holy and absolutely at peace. There was an ineffable glow about him.

I had intended to offer him a priesthood blessing if he wanted one. After watching him sleep for a few minutes, I decided to quietly sit down near his bed until he awakened. Suddenly he opened his eyes, as if he had sensed that someone was there. We talked for a while, and before I left I gave him a blessing, and then kissed him on the forehead.

A few days later I received the following letter from him; you will feel his spirit as you read it. Someone once said that compliments are not what we are, but what we *should* be. I will try to measure up to the kind things he wrote about me. His letter was the spiritual lift that carried me into the Christmas season.

> Dear Elder Featherstone,
>
> Thank you so much for taking time from your busy schedule to come and see me at the hospital. You truly are a great and humble man! I shall never forget opening my eyes and seeing you standing by my bed; nope, I'll never forget that experience.
>
> Thank you also for giving such a wonderful blessing. It helped me so much. I was thinking for the past several months about calling you and requesting a blessing, I even called your secretary

once, but you were overseas and wouldn't be back for a week, so I decided not to bother you. Then I opened my eyes, and there you were. Thank you!

I am recovering quite well. I feel pretty good, and my scar down my chest is healing really well. I figure that in four to six weeks I can get back to work again.

May the Lord continue to bless you and your family. Have a Merry Christmas! I love you very much. Again, thanks for everything.

Love, Dave

You only need one letter like that to give you the Christmas spirit! Kind and gentle words mean so much more from those you love and respect most.

Within three days of receiving that precious letter from David Harvey, I received another letter—this one from a woman that I didn't even think considered me her friend. Though it is brief, it represents more to me than anyone could ever know.

Over the years, I believe I have spent at least a thousand hours talking to this woman. She had lived alone most of her life, and since I didn't think anyone would give her a gift for Christmas, I had tried to provide gifts for her from money that has been given to me. During the Christmas season—over those many years, as well as now—I find my thoughts turning to her.

This was certainly not the only letter I had ever received from her. She wrote to me many times—sometimes finding fault, sometimes expressing suspicion, sometimes emotionally cold. She always addressed her letters to Vaughn Featherstone, D.B.C.G. For many years, I wondered what those initials meant. But the year she was eighty-five, this is the letter she sent to me that Christmas season:

> Dear Vaughn:
>
> Thank you for the lovely Christmas gift and your beautiful letter and note. I treasure them all deeply. Thank you, dear friend.
>
> Your letter and note are a special blessing to me at this Christmas season. The record and tapes are a spiritual feast I will enjoy throughout the years.
>
> God bless and keep you in His loving care always.
>
> Merry Christmas and Happy New Year.
>
> Love, P.P.

This woman recently passed away, but not before revealing what those mysterious initials meant. In one of her letters she spelled out the words she had abbreviated as "D.B.C.G."—her salutation to me, regardless of the tone of her letters, was "Dear Beloved Child of God." It touched my heart and filled my bucket to overflowing.

Francois-René de Chateaubriand said, "In the days of service, all things are founded; in the days of special privilege, they deteriorate; and in the days of vanity, they are destroyed."

Christmas is expressed through service and love. A good friend of mine, Charlie Davis, shared with me a story that should be repeated often; it was published in the December 21, 1977, issue of *The Press*.

The Gift
by Gary Acevedo

I remember it was the same year my father had lost his job. He had lacked work for a long time, enough to leave me with memories of using candles, because they had cut off our electricity. Even my only sweater bore holes, and my socks resembled Swiss cheese. We had never really been poor, but the hurdles of the past year had left us quite bad off. The neighbors offered help, but Dad was proud. He refused charity. I couldn't understand the whole situation, and it seemed to me that my smaller brother, Jerry, who had mowed lawns all summer long, owned 80 percent of the family's wealth. The money sat in a big piggy bank on top of his dresser drawers. Every once in a while, I'd sneak in and grab a little; I mean, he couldn't exactly be saving for college. Not in his condition, he wasn't.

You see, Jerry, who was a year younger than I was—twelve—was different from other people. He entered this world a mongoloid [person with Down's syndrome]. He looked different in a funny kind of way and had the mentality of a six-year-old. He also had a speech problem. His voice was real low and gruff, and he'd pronounce a lot of syllables wrong.

The difference had separated us, like weeds separate flowers. Yet, we used to be so close, when we were very young like baby cubs, climbing the tree of life. We laughed together, we cried together, we even stumbled together. I had learned to understand Jerry and couldn't detect any difference because we had stuck so closely together, being under our mother's wing.

But as the years came, along with other friends and children, so came the realization of his difference. It was becoming noticeable. Reality had whispered louder and louder that Jerry was different. His difference was an illness, a disease that took him from me, changed him continuously until he was no longer my brother, instead a simple animal. An inhuman thing that caused me enough embarrassment to make me hate him. Often I became cruel towards him.

I remember one time I'd gone to play some ball and as usual he'd shadowed right behind me. They wouldn't let me play because in order to keep the two teams equal, they'd only let two boys join in at a time. Nobody wanted Jerry, that kept me from playing too. It had happened many times before. Each time resentment mounted. Each time I hated him. There wasn't a moment that went by without him getting in the way. This time the mountain of hate exploded and I turned on him. "Look, you stupid lookin' creep. Why ya' gotta' follow me around? Leave me alone and go home." Then I slapped him, again and again, 'cause I wished he was dead. I couldn't go anywhere without being embarrassed. Everyone always referring to me as "the one with the M.R. for a brother." I didn't want to be embarrassed. I wished he was dead. He finally went home crying. I didn't care. I was too worried about the chewing out I'd be getting when I got home. Later on I really felt sorry for what I'd done. I felt even worse when I got home and discovered he hadn't told on me. Instead he came up to me and apologized to me for making me mad.

I also remember one time that summer we'd gone to the beach. Naturally I had to look out for Jerry, but all the kids started looking at us when they noticed Jerry was different. I couldn't take it, and I knew that if I ignored him long enough he'd get lost. Only he got lost for a long time. They'd begun to think he'd drowned. Pitifully enough, I couldn't have cared less. Hours later, an old man brought him back on top of his shoulders and said he'd found him about two miles down the beach, behind an old outhouse, sitting in the sand crying. You know, it seemed he did an awful lot of crying.

Well, as time passed, leaves fell, and snow came, everyone looked toward Christmas. I was looking at a dream. There was this beautiful watch in the jeweler's window. A watch with a gold band. It really wasn't too expensive, but too expensive for us. I knew it was impossible, but I liked to imagine that Christmas morning would find me wearing it. Every time I passed the shop I would stare at it forever.

I woke up Christmas morning rushing to open the one gift that was for me by the fireplace. It was a great looking sweater. I really needed one, too. "Thanks a lot, Dad," I shouted, but noticed how tired he looked so I asked him, "Did you stay up all night with Jerry again?" "Yes," he replied, "He's getting worse." You see, about a week before, Jerry and I had gone tubing. Jerry ended up at the bottom of the hill, head down, in the snowdrift. He lay there kicking and yelling for help, but again memories of the past embarrassing situations brought out my cruelty, and I watched him actually dying until I was satisfied. When I finally dug him out, instead of realizing what I had done, the poor dumb kid, between his gasps for air and his tears, tried to thank me for saving his life. Anyway, he caught pneumonia, and my parents had spent the last two nights with him.

"Let's go join your mother and Jerry," Dad said. Jerry's room smelled of medicine, and Jerry really looked horrible, but his eyes were all lit up. I didn't know why cause he was kinda' smilin', but Mother had been crying. She sniffed softly and said, "Jerry's got a surprise for you, Jim." I figured he was gonna' hit me with another one of his homemade, butcher-paper, water-colored type Christmas cards he'd made. He tried to jump out of bed but soon found he was so weary he could barely move. He wobbled over to his closet and pulled it out. Another card; just a flat sheet about a square foot big, and written in red watercolor, "To My Big Brother Whom I love the Most."

While I was reading it I noticed the broken pieces of his piggy bank in the corner. Then he slowly reached under his bed and pulled out a small box. He wiped his nose with his pajama sleeve, then stood there with his arm stretched out. His eyes lit up and with all the love he could muster up in the low gruff voice, he said, "Warwy Kwishmash, Shimmy!" I opened the box and there it was—gleaming, reflecting the snowflakes through the window—the watch, the beautiful watch with the gold band, the one I thought I'd never see again. I couldn't even stop looking at it. Then he gave me a bear hug and asked, "Shimmy, where my pweshent?" I looked up at him, over at the broken pieces of his bank in the corner, the watch, then back at the questioning eyes, and I didn't even have the courage to tell him I'd forgotten about him. I just grabbed him and started bawling like a baby. He never lived to say "Happy New Year." He died two days later.

It's Christmas Eve again; snowing again, too. I'd just gotten off the phone (parents called to say Merry Christmas). I laid back down on my dorm bed (I'm in college now). I laid down with my arms folded behind me and started to look at the only object on the wall; an old, homemade, water-colored, Christmas card. I checked the time on my watch—the one with the gold band, just a few seconds before midnight. I gazed up at the wall again and read the words aloud, "Whom I love the Most." Then . . . I could actually hear him say it again, "Warwy Kwishmash, Shimmy." Only this time I answered back as loud as I could, "Merry Christmas, Jerry, Merry Christmas."

Thank goodness we are able to remove from our pasts many unkind deeds that were done when we were young or immature. Frances Cornford wrote: "Why do you walk through the fields in gloves missing so much and so much? O [thoughtless] woman whom nobody loves why do you walk through the fields in gloves? When the grass is as soft as the breast of doves and shivering sweet to the touch? Why do you walk through the fields in gloves missing so much and so much?"

Christmas each year is different. We grow, we learn, we change, and hopefully we become more Christlike. I join with you this season in saying with all the love in my heart, "Merry Christmas, Jerry."

THE CHRISTMAS SPIRIT CARRIES ON

The brilliant star and tolling bell,
    A Christmas tree, the first noel,
A winter's night, the soft deep snow,
    Christmas carols, a fire's glow.

Of Him we think, the newborn Son,
    God's priceless gift to everyone;
A manger bed, a lowly stall,
    Where Jesus lay, the Lord of all.

The Holy Prince, the mother fair,
    And Joseph knelt as though in prayer;
The shepherds shy, the wise men knew
    The miracles God's Son would do.

On this holy Christmas night,
    The angels sweet and fair and bright,
Would sing hosannas to this child
    Of royal birth, yet meek and mild.

Millenniums have come and gone,
    But the Christmas spirit carries on,
And will as long as time shall be
    Our Savior for eternity.

CLOSER TO CHRIST AT CHRISTMAS

As a Church, we understand some things that the rest of the world does not. One of those things is the resplendent event celebrated each Christmas season—a season that, for us, revolves primarily around the Savior. While the rest of the world becomes caught up in stringing lights that outshine the neighbors and searching for the most lavish gifts, most of us remember that the center of Christmas is Christ.

The birth of the Savior was foretold by prophets, and the faithful believers were watching for the signs. Samuel the Lamanite described that night, predicting that "there shall be great lights in heaven, insomuch that in the night before he cometh there shall be no darkness, insomuch that it shall appear unto man as if it was day. . . . And behold, there shall a new star arise, such an one as ye have never beheld . . . [and] there shall be many signs and wonders in heaven" (Helaman 14:3, 5-6).

Nephi, the son of Helaman, was visited by the voice of the Lord, who declared, "Lift up your head and be of good cheer; for behold, the time is at hand, and on this night shall the sign be given, and on the morrow come I into the world . . ." (3 Nephi 1:13).

And centuries before the Savior's birth, Isaiah proclaimed, "For unto us a child is born, unto us a son is given: and the government shall be upon his shoulder: and his name shall be called Wonderful, Counsellor, The mighty God, The everlasting Father, The Prince of Peace" (Isasiah 9:6).

In trying to keep my heart focused on the simple reality of Christ as the center of Christmas, I like to think about the shepherds who watched their flocks along the hills surrounding Bethlehem more than two thousand years ago. I wonder if all of us, too, beheld that night from the other side of the veil and saw those shepherds scattered along the rocky outcroppings. Somehow I visualize a clear night sky, calm and vaulted by stars. In the heavens there must have been incredible anticipation, waiting for the final labor pains that would usher God's Only Begotten Son into a world in such desperate need. But the shepherds, who wandered silently through that quiet night, could not have imagined what was about to happen; some, eyelids heavy with fatigue, likely fought off sleep as they watched and guarded their sheep.

Suddenly, the star burst forth in splendid brilliance, lighting the night sky. It must have been both a terrible and glorious moment—both beast and man instantly recognizing that things would never again be the same, yet not understanding why. Imagine the dedicated shepherds, torn between watching their flocks and watching the star; feel, if you might, the fear that gradually overcame the awe as they struggled to protect their flocks.

Imagine then the incomprehensible moment when angels appeared in the now-bright sky. Could there have been a moment of terror? How quickly, though, were their souls drenched with inexpressible joy when they heard choirs of angels accompanying the heavenly announcement:

The Light of Hope

Fear not: for, behold, I bring you good tidings of great joy, which shall be to all people.

For unto you is born this day in the city of David a Saviour, which is Christ the Lord. . . .

And suddenly there was with the angel a multitude of heavenly host praising God, and saying,

Glory to God in the highest, and on earth peace, good will toward men" (Luke 2:10-14).

What a scene that must have been! That small group of shepherds must have stood in awe at the resplendence of the star and the heavenly hosts—sights they never could have imagined, sounds they had never before heard. How can you capture in words the rapture they must have felt? They were believers before this holy night, and they have been witnesses ever after.

Moving in the direction of the magnificent star, the humble shepherds were first to kneel before the Christ child. What a moment! Imagine Mary, having passed safely through her ordeal, her countenance radiant, a suffusion of holy light emanating from within. Nephi, who beheld Mary in vision, described her as a "virgin . . . exceedingly fair and white . . . most beautiful and fair above all other virgins" (1 Nephi 11:13, 15). She was even more beautiful in the moment the shepherds arrived, as is any mother who has just ushered a soul into this life. As they knelt near her to worship the Savior, they must have been overwhelmed by her purity, her beauty, and her innocence. As the shepherds knelt in the humble manger, Mary must have realized that they were not alone—that all of the hosts of heaven and earth bowed in reverence that night. How do you record such happenings except in the heart and mind? These are the kinds of events that cannot be described by tongue or pen.

Perhaps the closest we come to capturing the feelings of that sacred night is in the music we sing and hear at Christmas. With the heralding angels, we also shout, "Joy to the world, the Lord is come, let earth receive her King!" In reverence we sing, "O little town of Bethlehem, how still we see thee lie." We celebrate John MacFarlane's sentiments, "Far, far away on Judea's plains, shepherds of old heard the joyous strains." How often we have sung the simple words, "Away in a manger, no crib for his bed, the little Lord Jesus laid down his sweet head; the stars in the heaven looked down where he lay, the little Lord Jesus asleep on the hay." And there is a special, quiet reverence in Franz Gruber's beautiful music, "Silent night, holy night . . . Christ the Savior is born."

The music of Christmas helps bring us closer to Christ . . . and reminds us that He is the center of Christmas. The written word also has the power to bring our remembrance to the Savior. All of us recall "The Other Wise Man," the touching story by Henry Van Dyke. We relate to the messages in such works as "Conrad the Cobbler," "The Search for the Holy Grail," and "Gift of the Magi." The inspiring story of Handel composing *The Messiah* is recounted from year to year. These tender compositions by poets, authors, and musicians help us draw closer to Christ at Christmas.

For some, Christ comes only at Christmas. For us, He comes silently, softly, profoundly every day of our lives. We understand His role in the Godhead; we know that His place is on the right hand of God. We know that He is the Only Begotten of the Father in the flesh, and we struggle to understand the implications of that role. We know He is omnipotent, omniscient, and omnipresent.

We know much, much more about the Savior—but the things He has done (and continues to do) are the things that have touched me most deeply. How is it possible to consider His Atonement without being humbled to the dust? His suffering and death in the Garden and on the cross are incomparable acts. I am so moved to consider His tenderness with the widow of Nain, the woman with an issue of blood, and the Canaanite woman; His dealings with the lame, blind, and leprous; His compassion toward the widow and her mite. I glory at the account of His appearance to 2,500 souls at the temple in the land Bountiful, and His profound blessing of the children there. I weep over His encouragement to the Prophet Joseph in Liberty Jail. And I offer profound gratitude for the personal experiences in which He has touched my own life.

I reverence Him for who He is and all that carries with it—but I love Him with all my heart for what He has done and continues to do. I am so grateful for His mercy. I am grateful He has been there during the most trying times of my life. He has tolerated a lot of my nonsense and mistakes. He has endured my weaknesses and follies—and through them all, I have never doubted His love.

He is my light. He is *our* light. He is the eternal light and the hope of the world—and the center of all that is Christmas.

A CRADLE FOR CHRISTMAS

The second year we presided over the mission in San Antonio, Texas, we had a unique experience. We had invited President Spencer W. Kimball to come to San Antonio if he was near our area and had a spare day. It looked like he was going to be able to visit, so we worked out a date, notified all the missionaries and stake presidents, and made all the necessary plans.

We bought a pair of Texas longhorns to present to President Kimball; they were eight feet, nine inches long from one tip to the other. On the leather band holding the horns together, we embossed the words, "President Spencer W. Kimball." Below his name we embossed the name of the mission followed by words from President Kimball that had become our mission motto: "Make no small plans. They have no magic to stir men's souls."

All was ready for the prophet's visit.

Due to unavoidable conflicts, President Kimball was not able to come. We packed the longhorns in end-to-end bicycle boxes and shipped them to him in Salt Lake City. Arthur Haycock, the president's personal secretary, said it was the largest package they ever received.

When I arrived for General Conference that October, the security guard in the Church Administration Building told me that President Kimball wanted to see me as soon as I arrived. I went to his office. "Go right in," Brother Haycock told me, "the prophet is expecting you." As I entered President Kimball's private office, I immediately saw the Texas longhorns in the window—with about an inch and a half to spare on either end.

Sweet President Kimball got up, came over, and hugged me. It was a thrill. Then he said, "You wanted me to come to Texas. Would you still like me to do that?"

"President Kimball, we would give anything to have you come," I replied.

"Go sit down with Arthur, reserve some dates, and I will come," he said.

Arthur Haycock and I reserved the first week in December for the prophet's visit. As soon as I left his office, I called to notify my assistants of the dates when President Kimball would be there. I asked them in turn to notify the missionaries so they could begin to "prepare for the prophet."

During the next seven weeks, the missionaries, stake leaders, and members prepared for the prophet. The most important preparation was spiritual: We asked every missionary to look into his or her own soul the way a prophet might and to remove any impurities, disobedience, violation of mission rules, or anything that would cause the spirit to withdraw from his or her life. The results were phenomenal. The mission was purged and cleansed.

The month before President Kimball's arrival, my wife took me into the living room of the mission home and asked, "Do you think that is carpet befitting a prophet?"

"I know the carpet is old and needs to be replaced, but I have checked this year's budget, and we don't have enough money for new carpet," I told her.

Merlene was not about to be swayed. "Why don't you pay for it from our savings, and then get reimbursed after the first of the year?" she suggested. So that's exactly what I did.

But Merlene didn't stop with the carpet. She took me from room to room, pointing out some areas that needed to be painted. She drew my attention to a few other needed repairs. Finally, taking me into the bedroom, she pointed to the bed and said, "Do you think this bedspread is appropriate for the prophet and his wife?"

"It's not bad," I said. "You and I sleep under it."

"But this is *the prophet and his wife,*" she stressed.

I smiled at her consternation. "Well, why don't you go buy a bedspread worthy of the prophet." Merlene wasted no time buying a bedspread she felt was worthy of the prophet.

Most of my time had been spent on spiritually preparing the missionaries for the prophet, so I had not paid much attention to the physical details. The Saturday morning before the prophet's scheduled Friday visit, Merlene took me outside and said, "How does the yard look?"

"Well, it looks nicer than any in the neighborhood," I replied.

Merlene then delivered her worthy-of-a-prophet comments, and I agreed that it could stand some work. As a family, we worked all morning, and by noon we had a lawn and yard appropriate for the prophet.

We cleaned up and went out to lunch. When we returned, an office elder said, "You need to call Elder Aldin Porter, the Regional Representative in Boise. Two of your sons have been in a head-on collision, and one of them is not expected to live."

Our hearts sank. I called Elder Porter and learned that our oldest son, Ron, had a fractured neck and serious knee injuries, but he was going to be all right. Our second son, Dave, was in intensive care; his back was broken, and his chest was crushed. He was still alive but was in a coma; doctors were not certain he would live. If he did, there was doubt he would ever walk again.

As soon as she heard the news, Merlene said, "I have to go home." I suggested we pray instead and ask the Lord what we should do. After the prayer, I said, "Merlene, he is in God's hands. If you leave the mission, it's like we don't trust God to take care of him. I won't go home, and you shouldn't go home. Let's put our heart and soul into the work and trust David to God."

President Kimball was due the next Friday. We thought we had done all we could to prepare for his visit, but when our sons were injured, we were humbled to the dust of the earth. Every particle of false pride, selfishness, and daily concern was swept from us. When President Kimball and his wife stepped off the plane, we truly were prepared.

You can imagine how wonderful he was and how glorious it was to have the prophet preside at a two-hour mission conference followed by a regional conference that night. Every missionary shook his hand, and I don't know of one that had not completely cleansed his or her life.

Sunday morning at breakfast, President Kimball again asked about our sons. When I said I was ready to call our son in the hospital, President Kimball said, "Let me talk to him after you do."

After I had talked to him for a minute, I said, "David, there is someone here who wants to talk to you." David could barely speak; it took great effort, and still all he could manage was a whisper.

President Kimball got on the phone and said, "David." David recognized his voice, and later told us the tears flowed freely. "David, this is President Kimball. We want you and your brother to know that the First Presidency and Twelve Apostles prayed for you in the temple Thursday." He then offered some comforting words and hung up.

We took the Kimballs to the airport so they could fly on to Florida. Before he boarded the plane, President Kimball took Merlene aside and said, "Sister Featherstone, you go to Boise and be with your son for a few days." The tears of gratitude for the thoughtfulness of a sensitive prophet gathered in her eyes.

During the month of December, I pondered what to get my wife for Christmas. I decided the thing she would want most that year would be to have our three sons and their companions come to Texas. I had just enough royalties from a book I had written to cover the costs of the trips, so I contacted them and asked if they would come for Christmas if I would pay their way. I asked the boys to not tell their mother—this was my Christmas gift to her, and I wanted it to be a surprise.

Dave was still in the hospital and had not yet walked. I asked if he thought he could come. He was hesitant as he replied, "I don't know if the doctor will release me by then." I sent him and his wife tickets for December 23, to arrive late in the afternoon. I thought it might be helpful for him to have a goal. The night before he was scheduled to fly, I called; he was still not sure the doctors would release him from the hospital in time to make the plane.

Our son Ron had arrived a couple of days earlier on a Saturday. Before his arrival, I had told Merlene and the rest of the family, "We need to go to the airport and pick up an elder." That was true . . . my son was an elder!

"Do we *have* to go along?" the kids groaned.

"Yes, it's Christmas," I reminded them, "and if this was your brother, you would want someone there to meet him."

There are seven military installations around San Antonio, and we walked through the airport where active-duty husbands and wives were meeting each other for Christmas. Our hearts swelled with emotion as we saw them run toward each other and embrace. Watching the scene, Merlene grew a little misty. "I would give anything in the world if my sons could be with us this Christmas," she whispered. I just about told her, but I was able to wait.

As those on the plane began to disembark, my excitement grew. Soon our son came out. He was on crutches as a result of the knee injuries sustained in the accident; his little son Christopher was walking beside him, and his wife was carrying our granddaughter Nicole. I turned to Merlene and said, "Merry Christmas."

"Thanks," she sighed, showing no signs of excitement. I was taken aback: I thought after spending that much money, my gift merited some tears. Then I wondered if one of the missionaries had spilled the beans and told her about my surprise. So I tried again: "Merlene, this is your Christmas gift—Merry Christmas!"

Merlene showed no special emotion. As it turned out, she was looking for a missionary and didn't even see her own son until he was standing right in front of her. She looked up, let out a little scream, burst into tears, and hugged him. *That* was more like it—more what I thought I had earned for that kind of an investment!

The Light of Hope

At that point I told her all three of her sons were coming, though David was questionable—he would make it if the doctors released him and if he could walk. The next day we had a wonderful Christmas zone conference, followed by a large Christmas dinner for all the missionaries that was served by one of the wards. While the rest of us ate, I sent the family out to the airport to pick up David and his wife in case they were able to make it.

The plane was due at 5 p.m. By 6:30, the family was still not back. I assumed that David had not been able to come, and that the family was busy checking out other possible flights he might have been on.

We had a beautiful Christmas program for the missionaries in the evening. One missionary read O'Henry's *The Gift of the Magi*. A soloist sang *O Holy Night*. Someone read a condensed version of *The Other Wise Man*. Together, we all sang carols. The Spirit filled the room, and I know everyone partook of its beauty.

As I was standing at the back of the cultural hall, one of the missionaries approached me and said, "President, I think your son is here." I went over to the door and looked down the hallway. My son David was walking toward me. I will never be able to express in words the love I had for the Lord at that instant—or the overwhelming feelings of gratitude that flooded my soul.

The next day I asked David if he had a Christmas gift for his wife.

"No, Dad, I don't," he said. "I came here straight from the hospital."

"Then let's go get one," I said. We drove to a large department store in downtown San Antonio; I turned to David and told him, "I know just the gift."

David and his wife had been married almost five years, and they had tried desperately to have children. David and I had given her blessings, but still the desired pregnancy did not occur. They had even contacted LDS Social Services and applied for adoption.

I pushed David's wheelchair to the furniture department, pointed to a beautiful wooden cradle, and said, "This is a great gift."

David's eyes grew misty, and his voice choked with emotion as he said, "Dad, we aren't even pregnant."

"I know you'd have to have a lot of faith to buy that for Laura," I said.

"It would hurt too much," he replied. "I just couldn't do it."

"Well, it was just an idea," I said, patting him on the shoulder.

We went to another department and were looking at other things when David suddenly stopped the wheelchair. "You're right, Dad," he said. "The cradle is the gift for her." We took it home Christmas Eve, and then I got up early Christmas morning to put the cradle out.

David was concerned about how Laura might react, and he didn't want her to be embarrassed in front of the entire family—so he got up at 5 a.m. and took Laura to the living room to see her gift. The minute she saw the beautiful wooden cradle, the tears came. They shared a tender moment and had a long talk. By the time the rest of the family came into the living room, Laura was composed.

A few days after Christmas, we loaded everyone on the plane—including the cradle.

Five weeks later, David called and said, "Dad, please get Mom on the phone." Once Merlene was on the extension,

David said, "I've got Laura on our extension. Social Services just called. They have twin boys for us! They were being cared for in a foster home until I had more completely recovered from the accident!"

I was humbled to tears as I thought of the great goodness of our God. Yes, we had purchased a cradle for Christmas, and now we had twin boys to share it.

Many years have passed, and the twins have returned from their missions—one served in Ecuador and the other in Brazil. Every Christmas is special in its own way, but none of us will ever forget the year we got a cradle for Christmas.

ON CHRISTMAS NIGHT

On Christmas night so long ago
    A tiny babe was born,
While angels sang both sweet and clear
    On that special morn.

One star shone clear and brilliant,
    And shepherds watched in awe.
And the lowing cattle all stood still
    While the sheep and donkey saw—

The infant child, a baby boy,
    The Son of God was born.
Mary cradled Him at her breast
    On that damp, chill morn.

An aura shone round 'bout him
    As he lay in swaddling clothes,
A halo shone o'er his tiny head;
    All who saw him said, "He glows."

The wise men from the East did bring
    Frankincense, myrrh, and gold,
While a great light shone on Mary
    And the Christ child she did hold.

Generations now have passed away
    Since the heavens proclaimed the king,
And a thousand million Christians
    Worship Him as they sing—

"Glory to God in the highest,
    And on earth, good will to all";
Our Lord Jesus was born in a manger,
    He was sheltered in a stall.

Ring out, ye bells, for Christ is born,
    The Prince of Peace has come,
Glad tidings peal from heaven's dome
    And through all Christendom.

THE DEAR CHRIST ENTERS IN

Soon after my wife and I were married, I was called on a stake mission just as the Christmas season approached. My companion—S. Eugene England, Sr.—had been called to serve as a mission president in the Midwest but had been asked to keep the call confidential. He was interested in gaining as much experience as possible before he reported for his assignment as mission president, so he had volunteered to serve as a stake missionary. I had no idea he was preparing to be a mission president, but dutifully reported for weekly meetings in his home.

The night of our first meeting it was snowing; my old 1937 Plymouth was not running, so I walked the three or four blocks to his home through the snow. I was wearing the only coat I owned—a wool overcoat someone had given me. The outside of the coat looked pretty good, but the lining was in pretty rough condition.

President England welcomed me at his door. He offered to help me off with my coat, and I held my arms close together as he slid it off so he would not see the lining. He took my coat and hung it up in a closet.

He led me to the living room, where everyone had gathered. His home was beautiful! The rich carpeting was an elegant gray-blue color, and a large oil painting hung over a magnificent marble fireplace. There were beautiful lamps, a large elegant sofa and chair, and stunning accent pieces. Everything in his home was wonderful, and a sweet spirit abided there.

His wife was a lovely woman—refined, warm, and hospitable. She attended to her husband's every need and was helpful to each one of us. I listened carefully to President England and watched the way he treated his wife. I continued to study the beauty of their home. I don't think I got much out of the meeting as far as missionary instruction; my mind was occupied with Gene England, his wife, and their lovely home. I remember thinking that I wanted to treat my wife the way Gene England treated his wife. I wanted to have my wife love and respect me like his wife did him. I wanted to have a wonderful home with well-appointed furnishings like they had. Those were my goals that night.

As the meeting drew to a close, it was still snowing outside. I went to the closet to get my coat, and it was missing. I thought, "He probably looked at the lining and decided to throw it away." I acted like I hadn't brought a coat and tried to slip out quietly so no one would notice I didn't have on an overcoat.

Suddenly President England was standing behind me, helping me on with my overcoat. I slipped one arm in without incident, but when I put my second arm into the sleeve, it slipped between the coat and the lining. The end of the lining was securely sewed to the sleeve, and I couldn't get my hand out of the end of the sleeve. I would have given *anything* if I could have forced my hand on through.

Finally I turned to President England and I said, "I'm sorry; my arm went between the coat and the lining." His countenance was so kind as he let me pull my arm out of the coat, get it in the sleeve as it should be, and slip the coat completely on. I thanked him for his kindness and left.

Edgar A. Guest wrote a poem, "The Inn-Keeper Makes Excuses," that beautifully illustrates the contrast between the innkeeper at Bethlehem and my host, Gene England. On that wintry night, I felt like a tramp who was invited into a royal setting—yet there was never a word said about my shabby coat. Instead, I was treated with dignity, kindness, and appreciation. Keep that contrast in mind as you read the words to the poem:

> "Oh, if only I had known!"
>   Said the keeper of the inn.
> "But no hint to me was shown,
>   And I didn't let them in.
>
> "Yes, a star gleamed overhead,
>   But I couldn't read the skies,
> And I'd given every bed
>   To the very rich and wise.
>
> "And she was so poorly clad,
>   And he hadn't much to say!
> But no room for them I had,
>   So I ordered them away.
>
> "She seemed tired, and it was late
>   And they begged so hard, that I
> Feeling sorry for her state,
>   In the stable let them lie.

"Had I turned some rich man out
    Just to make a place for them,
'Twould have killed, beyond a doubt,
    All my trade in Bethlehem.

"Then there came the wise men three
    To the stable, with the morn
Who announced they'd come to see
    The great King who had been born.

"And they brought Him gifts of myrrh,
    Costly frankincense and gold,
And a great light shone on her
    In the stable, bleak and cold.

"All my patrons now are dead
    And forgotten, but to-day
All the world to peace is led
    By the ones I turned away.

"It was my unlucky fate
    To be born that Inn to own,
Against Christ I shut my gate—
    Oh, if only I had known!"

As I walked home in the snow that night, I was a changed man. I had seen things far better than I had, and I had made a decision: I was going to try to be like him, and I was going to have a wonderful home like his.

The Light of Hope

At that time we had two little boys and I was doing well at my job, but we did not have a lot of extra cash. That Christmas most of our discretionary money was spent on our boys' gifts. I did get my wife an elegant white leather-bound triple combination with her name inscribed in gold on the cover. She wept with appreciation when she unwrapped it. She gave me a new set of temple robes and clothing. I was overcome. Gene England's home was still elegant and much finer than what I had—but I could not have cherished any more the simple but meaningful gifts exchanged in our little family. That day, as on many days since then, the Christmas spirit filled our modest home to overflowing.

The Christmas spirit requires a believing heart, a grateful heart, and Christlike compassion. Filled with that spirit, we extend beyond our inner selves—and, as a result, our problems, trials, perplexities, and troubles seem to fade. Those challenges don't go away, but steeped in joy that accompanies the true spirit of Christmas, we are able to put them in their proper perspective.

I have often wondered what kind of Christmas we could create if we could not spend money—not only the money we spend for gifts, but the money we spend on decorations and all the other trappings of the holiday. I suspect that our focus during the Christmas season would be on spending time with family, singing carols, reading from the scriptures, attending church, and caring for those in need. We would probably spend more time gathered around the dinner table than searching for gifts under the tree. Letters would likely be written to loved ones, expressing our fondest and most tender feelings. Homemade gifts would require creativity, time, and effort—and would almost certainly be deeply appreciated.

When I was in the second grade, we made gifts for our parents at Christmas. Our teacher had us cut out a little cardboard man about ten inches tall; working as though it was a rear view, we pasted on hair, a shirt, a pair of pants, and shoes crafted from colored paper. Finally, we pasted a patch of sand paper across the seat of his pants. A little sign adhered to his back read, "Scratch your match on my patch!" We had a gas stove, and my mother kept that little cardboard tramp hanging on a hook by the stove for almost twenty years. It was the only thing I could afford to give her at the time, but she treated it as a priceless gift.

The greatest gift of all isn't displayed in the sparkling window of a department store or printed on the glossy pages of a magazine or catalog. It can't be purchased with money. It is the sequence of events that took place on that dark, still night in Bethlehem when Mary wrapped her infant in swaddling clothes and laid Him in a manger . . . when Joseph, a humble carpenter, stood sentinel over God's own Son . . . when shepherds left their fields and came to worship the Christ child.

The world may not believe, but we know; they may not care, but we bow in reverence; they may deny, but we testify to the world that the Messiah, the long-awaited Prince of Peace, is indeed the King of Kings. And in the hearts of believers, the dear Christ enters in—the center and focus of all that is Christmas.

THE GIFT OF CHRISTMAS LETTERS

One Christmas years ago I was invited to speak at my home ward. At that time our ward had nearly a dozen full-time missionaries in the field. As I thought about my assignment, I was prompted with a way I could add great spiritual dimension to the meeting: I wrote to all of the full-time missionaries and asked each to write a Christmas letter that I could read to the members of the ward.

Every single missionary responded with a beautiful Christmas letter. Every letter was magnificent, filled with the Spirit that is so unique to missionaries, especially at this time of year. I don't think there was a dry eye in the chapel when I shared those letters—especially among the families who heard the words of their sweet sons and daughters.

One of the letters was from John Weaver who was serving in Haiti. I traveled extensively during my twenty-eight years as a General Authority, and nowhere I visited rivaled the poverty that exists in Haiti. Elder Weaver wrote:

> While being here in Haiti I've been aware of just how blessed I am, probably because of the striking contrast I see all around me. It's very difficult to

try to explain conditions down here because you just can't believe or understand it until you've seen it and lived in it. Maybe I can share an experience that can explain my feelings of gratitude.

I worked in an area in the heart of Port-au-Prince called Demas. Within my area was the place nicknamed the "Pit"—not because of the lack of success there, but because of the extreme poverty. All of the houses were cinderblock boxes with tin roofs and an occasional cement floor. We usually didn't do a whole lot of teaching in the "Pit" because most of the people resented us "rich foreigners."

One night after a discussion we were walking back home with a member, and we decided to take a shortcut through the "Pit." On our way through we were stopped by a young girl who looked as though she was going to beg from us. She was standing there with one good leg bearing up most of the weight of her body and the other, only half as long, twisted and deformed, slipped into a makeshift brace. The brace was made out of rebar with a metal plate welded to the bottom and a child's shoe tied to a crossbar halfway up so she could slip her distorted foot into it for support. My companion and I expected her to ask us for some money or food, but much to our surprise she wanted to know about the gospel.

The Light of Hope

We were more than happy to set an appointment with her, but we still had a sneaking hunch she was after a handout of some kind. It needs to be known that the other churches here give everything away—from Bibles (that most people can't read) to educations, from food and clothing to shelter. All of those things are very important, but unfortunately people become very dependent on handouts. We were afraid that's what Josianne was after.

When we went to our scheduled appointment with her, we found her out on the side of the main road waiting for us. After a brief greeting, she turned and slowly and painfully to be sure, led us on a ten-minute walk back to the very depths of the "Pit." Her house was made of cinderblock; about twenty feet square, it was split into two rooms. Later I found out that there were five adults and two children living in these two rooms.

Josianne proved to be very bright, well educated for her circumstances, and very religious. Each time we taught a lesson she was very eager to learn and study and pray about it. Her testimony would be bigger every time we went back. After the first invitation to come to church, she was there regularly to all the meetings.

If I remember right, she accepted a baptismal challenge after the second discussion. We could hardly believe how fast she was progressing. Later on I discovered that her growth had been in direct proportion to her sacrifices. While I thought she was riding a Tap Tap (Haitian public transportation) to church and back, she had been struggling to walk more than a mile over a rather large hill with her bad leg, each way.

Soon after she started taking the lessons, she told her pastor that she had found the **true church** and she would no longer be attending his church. The pastor promptly cut off all financial aid, making it impossible for her to pay for her school.

When her neighbor realized the Mormon missionaries were teaching her, he built a wall across the patio that she needed to cross to get to her house; he left only one small passageway, a gutter that was quite slick because of the moss that grew there. This narrow gutter between the structures was now her only means of access to her house. One day I noticed she was moving slower than usual and with greater pain than she was accustomed to. When I asked her why, she told me she had fallen in the entranceway and had bruised and sprained her already crippled leg. That explained her absence at church that morning—she had fallen on her way out and was hurt too badly to make the rest of the trip.

The day before I was transferred to Les Cayes, I had the privilege of baptizing Josianne. Needless to say it was one of the highlights of my mission thus far. The things that impressed me so much about Josianne were her great conviction and her willingness to do whatever was necessary to become a member of the ONLY TRUE CHURCH. Throughout all of her suffering, she never once complained or longed for sympathy. It makes one both grateful and humble to realize just how much people sacrifice to have what we have been given. Even though I'm a heck of a long ways from home, and I miss my family, particularly during this holiday season, I'm sure this will be one of my most memorable Christmases."

One link always holds, and one light will never go out. As long as we have missionaries in the field, such stories will be told.

One couple shared with me a letter they had received from their daughter and son-in-law. "We never could adequately express our love and feelings for you," they wrote. "You have been there for us at every turn. We have thought and thought about what we could give you this year for Christmas. We wanted it to be special and from our hearts." With love, they enclosed four checks to pay for the remaining months of their brother's mission, expressing gratitude at the opportunity to support him in his missionary labors. As you can imagine, the parents were incredibly touched.

Wouldn't that be a wonderful thing to do? Perhaps a quorum, class, or group of youth could cover a month or two of mission expenses for a family that is stretching to the limit to keep a missionary in the field. Maybe older sons who have served missions could offer to help with the expenses for a younger sibling who is now in the mission field. Oliver Goldsmith reaffirms, "The greatest object in the universe, says a certain philosopher, is a good man struggling with adversity; yet there is a still greater, which is the good man [or woman] that comes to relieve it" (*A New Dictionary of Quotations,* H. L. Mencken, 17).

A letter issued by the Royal Bank of Canada in June 1987 reflected on the traditions surrounding Christmas. In summation, the letter concluded, "At Christmas, we are positively obliged to drop the business of making a living and enjoy ourselves for a while. When we indulge in formality of this kind we come in touch with the finer things in life . . . and better selves enter a better world than the one we would normally inhabit."

Touching the true spirit of Christmas does allow us to touch the more precious things in life. Jim Clegg, a treasured friend who has since passed away, shared with me a wonderful experience that happened two decades ago when he was serving as a stake president. He was conducting a special Christmas fireside in his stake at which President Spencer W. Kimball was giving the Christmas message. Just before the meeting began, an unkempt young man with long hair and dirty clothes approached Jim at the pulpit, handed him a poem, and asked him to read it. Jim looked over the poem, then told the young man he would not read it as part of the meeting. The young man left the poem on the pulpit and returned to his seat.

Suddenly President Kimball tugged on Jim's jacket and asked to read the poem. After quietly reading the poem, he handed it back to Jim—and suggested that Jim honor the request. Jim Clegg read the following poem by an unknown author as part of his address:

The Little Black Dog
I wonder if Christ has a little black dog
All curly and woolly like mine,
With two silly ears and a nose round and wet
And two eyes, brown and tender, that shine.

I'm sure if He had, that little black dog
Knew right from the first He was God,
That he needed no proof that Christ was divine,
But just worshiped the ground that He trod.

I'm afraid that He hadn't, because I have read
How He prayed in the garden alone,
For all of His friends and disciples had fled
Even Peter, the one they called Stone.

And, oh, I'm sure that little black dog
With a heart so tender and warm,
Would never have left Him to suffer alone,
But creeping right under His arm
Would have licked those dear fingers
In agony clasped
And counted all favors but loss,
When they took Him away, would have trotted behind
And followed Him right to the cross.

What a sweet sentiment! We all get letters for Christmas, and in them we often find the most tender, thoughtful expressions penned by people who are filled with the Spirit. These letters, read and committed to the heart, can bless our Christmas seasons. In that hope, then, I offer my letter to each of you at this Christmas season:

Dear fellow lover of Jesus,

I hope that you have a spiritual Christmas filled with music and with the Spirit of Christ. It's all right if you don't get everything you want.

It is okay if you can't give everything you would like. You have each other . . . be kind, be good, be tender, be soft, but most of all be forgiving, and you will be better this year.

Remember He understands your heart and motives.

He understands every desperate feeling you experience.

He knows about those of you who have sons and daughters on missions and the longing you feel for them.

And He knows that you continue to pay your tithes and offerings.

He knows your service to the kingdom, your sacrifices to do His work, and the depth of your love for Him.

The Light of Hope

I think He would say to you, "You can make it. It's all right. I love you, and I will forgive you." I pray that you can feel a wave of absolution sweep over you and that you can have the sweet assurance that you are His—bought with His blood and cradled in His care.

Have a merry Christmas! Write a letter to someone you feel could use a spiritual lift and a warm greeting to a dear friend. Your simple words committed to paper may prove to be more important than you could ever suppose.

I love you and wish you the merriest of Christmases.

WHO TAKES THE SON GETS IT ALL

Sherman Lovelace, a good friend from Pasadena, Maryland, was kind enough to share the following story with me and has given me permission to share it now.

Take the Son

Years ago, there was a very wealthy man who, with his devoted young son, shared a passion for art collecting. Together they traveled around the world, adding only the finest art treasures to their collection.

Priceless works by Picasso, Van Gogh, Monet, and many others adorned the walls of the family estate.

The widowed older man looked on with satisfaction as his only child became an experienced art collector. The son's trained eye and sharp business mind caused his father to beam with pride as they dealt with art collectors around the world.

As winter approached, war engulfed the nation, and the young man left to serve his country. After only a few short weeks, his father received a telegram.

His beloved son was missing in action. The art collector anxiously awaited more news, fearing he would never see his son again. Within days, his fears were confirmed: The young man had died while rushing a fellow soldier to a medic.

Distraught and lonely, the old man faced the upcoming Christmas holidays with anguish and sadness. The joy of the season that he and his son had so looked forward to would visit his house no longer.

On Christmas morning, a knock on the door awakened the depressed old man. Having excused the servants for the Christmas holidays, he arose to answer the door. As he walked to the door, the masterpieces of art on the walls only reminded him that his son was not coming home. As he opened the door, he was greeted by a soldier with a large package in his hands.

He introduced himself to the man by saying, "I was a friend of your son. I was the one he was rescuing when he died. May I come in for a few moments? I have something to show you."

As the two began to talk, the soldier told of how the man's son had told everyone of his—not to mention his father's—love of fine art. "I am an artist," said the soldier, "and I want to give you this."

As the old man unwrapped the package, the paper gave way to reveal a portrait of the man's son. Though the world would never consider it the work of a genius, the painting featured the young man's face in striking detail.

Overcome with emotion, the man thanked the soldier, promising to hang the picture above the fireplace. A few hours after the soldier had departed, the old man set about his task. True to his word, the painting went above the fireplace, pushing aside thousands of dollars worth of art. His task completed, the old man sat in his chair and spent Christmas gazing at the gift he had been given.

During the days and weeks that followed, the man realized that even though his son was no longer with him, the boy's life would live on because of those he had touched. He would soon learn that his son had rescued dozens of wounded soldiers before a bullet stilled his caring heart.

As the stories of his son's gallantry continued to reach him, fatherly pride and satisfaction began to ease his grief. The painting of his son became his most prized possession, far eclipsing any interest in the pieces for which museums around the world clamored. He told his neighbors it was the greatest gift he had ever received.

The following spring, the old man became ill and passed away. The art world was in anticipation that with the collector's passing, and his only son dead, his paintings would be sold at auction. According to the will of the old man, all of the art works would be auctioned on Christmas Day, the day he had received his greatest gift.

The day soon arrived, and art collectors from around the world gathered to bid on some of the world's most spectacular paintings. Dreams would be fulfilled this day; greatness would be achieved as many would claim, "I have the greatest collection."

The auction began with a painting that was not on any museum's list. It was the painting of the man's son. The auctioneer asked for an opening bid, but the room was silent.

"Who will open the bidding with $100?" he asked. Minutes passed, and no one spoke. From the back of the room came a voice, "Who cares about the painting? It's just a picture of his son."

"Let's forget about it and move on to the good stuff," more voices echoed in agreement.

"No, we have to sell this one first," replied the auctioneer. "Now, who will take the son?" Finally, a neighbor of the old man spoke, "Will you take ten dollars for the painting? That's all I have. I knew the boy, so I would like to have it."

"I have ten dollars. Will anyone go higher?" called the auctioneer. After more silence, the auctioneer said, "Going once, going twice, gone."

Cheers filled the room and someone exclaimed, "Now we can get on with it and bid on the real treasures!"

The auctioneer looked at the audience and announced that the auction was over. Stunned disbelief quieted the room. Someone spoke up and asked, "What do you mean, it's all over? We didn't come here for a picture of some old guy's son. What about all of these paintings? There are millions of dollars worth of art there! I demand that you explain what's going on!"

The auctioneer replied, "It's very simple. According to the will of the father, whoever takes the son . . . gets it all."

From an eternal perspective, doesn't that direction ring true? The message that the art collectors discovered on Christmas Day is still the same.

Yes, whoever takes the Son of God gets it all. At Christmas we love to recount sweet stories reminiscent of the type of love that the Savior has for all. Our tendencies to be kind and soft approach the surface; we think holier thoughts, and we do kindlier things. Removing the blinders of jaded apathy, we see the needs of those around us. One of the purest acts of charity is performed by Christmas sentinels from the Salvation Army who awaken our need to bless others by ringing a little bell. At Christmastime we are inclined to reach out, and I believe God smiles in response. For a few short days, we gravitate toward heaven.

Somehow in the midst of all the sorrows and sicknesses in the world, there is a wondrous light of hope that shines on all of us. It is the Light of Christ, and once it has illuminated our souls, it never leaves. Jesus Christ is the Savior of all mankind—not just of Christians, but also of Buddhists and Moslems and the disciples of Confucius and Mohammad.

Because of Him, resurrection and everlasting life will come to all who walk the earth. Christmas reminds us that He is, the only true and living Son of the eternal God, and that His arms are outstretched to all mankind. He is the Author of charity, the pure love of Christ.

Through Him, hope springs eternally. His precious love is extended to all. Together with the Christian world we sing, "Joy to the world, the Lord is come." Oh, what a coming!

As we consider Christmas—a time of giving and receiving, of loving and forgiving—we consider the sweet assurance that to those of us who receive that Son, all will be given.

ABOUT THE AUTHOR

Elder Vaughn J. Featherstone was sustained as second counselor in the Presiding Bishopric of The Church of Jesus Christ of Latter-day Saints on April 6, 1972. He was sustained a member of the First Quorum of the Seventy on October 1, 1976. Elder Featherstone received Emeritus status in October 2001.

He has served as the Young Men general president, as president of the Texas San Antonio Mission, as president of the Logan Temple, as a member of the YMMIA General Board, as president of six areas of the Church, as stake president, and as a member of the Boy Scouts of America National Executive Board. Elder Featherstone has received the Silver Beaver, Silver Antelope, Silver Buffalo, and Distinguished Eagle Scout awards.

Before being called as a General Authority, Elder Featherstone was a corporate training manager for a major supermarket chain based in Boise, Idaho.

Elder Featherstone was born in Stockton, Utah, to Stephen E and Emma M. Johnson Featherstone. He and his wife, Merlene, are the parents of seven children.